EVERYTHING series!

THESE HANDY, accessible books give you all you need to tackle a difficult project, gain a new hobby, comprehend a fascinating topic, prepare for an exam, or even brush up on something you learned back in school but have since forgotten.

You can read an EVERYTHING® book from cover to cover or just pick out the information you want from our four useful boxes: e-facts, e-ssentials, e-alerts, and e-questions. We literally give you everything you need to know on the subject, but throw in a lot of fun stuff along the way, too.

We now have well over 300 EVERYTHING® books in print, spanning such wide-ranging topics as weddings, pregnancy, wine, learning guitar, one-pot cooking, managing people, and so much more. When you're done reading them all, you can finally say you know EVERYTHING®!

Ⓔ **Facts:** Important sound bytes of information

Ⓔ **Essentials:** Quick and handy tips

Ⓔ **Alerts:** Urgent warnings

Ⓔ **Questions:** Solutions to common problems

THE
EVERYTHING®
Series

Dear Reader,

Bonjour! Thanks for taking a look at *The Everything® French Phrase Book*, my first French book. I've been a "virtual French teacher" since 1999, when I began working as the French Guide at About.com. My site, ✑*http://french.about.com*, is widely considered the best Web site for the French language, with 2,500+ pages of free resources for students, teachers, and lovers of French.

I've been obsessed with French ever since I was ten or eleven, and my brother taught me to count. My original dream was to be a conference interpreter, and although that particular objective was never realized, what I do now is just as interesting and valuable. Working freelance also makes it easy to travel—I've been to France numerous times and have lived there twice (six weeks in Rouen and two months in Paris). I've also visited Belgium and Switzerland, and lived in Morocco for two and a half years. So now that you know a little bit about me, it's time for you to get cracking with some French phrases. *Allons-y!*

Laura Lawless

THE
EVERYTHING®
FRENCH PHRASE BOOK

A quick reference for any situation

Laura K. Lawless

Adams Media
Avon, Massachusetts

Pour mes belles nièces, Danielle Nicole et Allie Justine.
J'espère qu'un jour, vous en aurez besoin !
• • •

An Everything® Series Book.
Everything® and everything.com are registered trademarks of
F+W Publications, Inc.

Published by Adams Media, an F+W Publications Company
57 Littlefield Street, Avon, MA 02322 U.S.A.
www.adamsmedia.com

ISBN: 1-59337-144-6

Printed in Canada.

J I H G F E D C B

Library of Congress Cataloging-in-Publication Data
Lawless, Laura K.
The everything French phrase book / Laura K. Lawless.
p.   cm.
(Everything series book)
English and French.
ISBN 1-59337-144-6
1. French language--Conversation and phrase books--English.
I. Title. II. Series: Everything series.

PC2121.L417 2005
448.3'421--dc22

2004013354

This publication is designed to provide accurate and authoritative information
with regard to the subject matter covered. It is sold with the understanding that
the publisher is not engaged in rendering legal, accounting, or other professional
advice. If legal advice or other expert assistance is required, the services of a com-
petent professional person should be sought.

—From a *Declaration of Principles* jointly adopted by a Committee of the
American Bar Association and a Committee of Publishers and Associations

Many of the designations used by manufacturers and sellers to distinguish their
products are claimed as trademarks. Where those designations appear in this
book and Adams Media was aware of a trademark claim, the designations have
been printed with initial capital letters.

Cover illustrations by Barry Littmann.

This book is available at quantity discounts for bulk purchases.
For information, call 1-800-872-5627.

THE
EVERYTHING®
Series

EDITORIAL

Publishing Director: Gary M. Krebs
Managing Editor: Kate McBride
Copy Chief: Laura MacLaughlin
Acquisitions Editor: Eric M. Hall, Gina Marzilli
Development Editor: Julie Gutin
Production Editor: Jamie Wielgus
Language Editor: Susana C. Schultz

PRODUCTION

Production Director: Susan Beale
Production Manager: Michelle Roy Kelly
Series Designer: Daria Perreault
Cover Design: Paul Beatrice and Matt LeBlanc
Layout and Graphics: Colleen Cunningham,
Rachael Eiben, Michelle Roy Kelly,
John Paulhus, Daria Perreault, Erin Ring

Acknowledgments

Thanks again to Barb Doyen and Eric Hall, my agent and editor, respectively. It really does get easier! Huge thanks to my big brother Timmy for inadvertently setting me off on a life full of language by teaching me to count in French.

À Martine, Marie, Alan, Charlyne, Gail, Stella, Walter et mes autres hôtes, merci mille fois pour votre assistance, ces dernières années, et bises à tous mes amis qui font partie de la communauté À la française.

And of course my husband, Orin, deserves many thanks for always being there for me—except when I didn't want him. Writing a book is hard work, as is living with someone who is writing a book. Thanks for your nearly endless patience.

Mille fois merci à toutes et à tous !

Contents

Introduction

Learning French is not the easiest thing in the world, but it can be extremely interesting and worthwhile. Whether you want to visit French-speaking countries, interact with native speakers in your community, or just learn more about the world we live in, being able to speak French will definitely make the experience more enjoyable. Speaking French does more than open up a new means of communication; it can also help you to understand more about Francophone people and cultures, because language and culture go hand in hand.

French is a Romance language; since Romance languages are all descended from Latin, they have many similarities. If you have already studied another Romance language, you will find that some French concepts are very easy for you because you already learned about them when studying another language.

French is spoken in France, Belgium, Switzerland, some Caribbean islands, the South Pacific, parts of Canada, and much of West Africa, as well as in several immigrant communities in the United States and around the world. There are numerous variations in grammar, vocabulary, and pronunciation both between and within French-speaking regions. If this seems strange to you, think about the many differences between and within American, British, Canadian, and Australian English and the various difficulties you experience when speaking and/or listening to English speakers from other regions. In the same way, there may be some confusion when you talk to French speakers from different countries, but you should be able to communicate with Francophones wherever you go without too much difficulty, even if the French you learned is from another region.

The three main sections in *The Everything® French Phrase Book* are lessons, phrases, and appendices. You should start with the lessons, which are not exhaustive, but which teach you the most important aspects of French grammar and pronunciation. Chapter 1 is an introduction to French and some of the similarities and differences between French and English, while Chapter 2 teaches you basic French grammar. After studying these chapters, you will understand a bit more about French grammar, vocabulary, and pronunciation, and why things are said the way they are.

Chapters 3 through 14 consist of French phrases for every situation. Each French phrase is accompanied by an English translation and an approximate English pronunciation. English words which use the same spelling for that pronunciation are provided whenever possible. When there is no real English equivalent, the nearest sound, if any, is explained in parentheses—for these letters and letter combinations, see Chapter 1.

The phrase book ends with three appendices: a French/English dictionary, an English/French dictionary, and a list of recommended resources for further information about French language and culture.

The Everything® French Phrase Book is designed to help you in two ways: It offers an introduction to the most important French grammar concepts and pronunciation difficulties, and it provides useful phrases for common travel situations. With the introduction out of the way, turn the page to start learning more about French.

Chapter 1
Introduction to French

French is a Romance language; in contrast, English belongs to the Germanic family. In theory, French and English should be very distinct languages, but in reality, there is German influence in French and Latin influence in English, not to mention a fair amount of French in English and vice versa. This means the two languages share a number of similarities. This chapter is an introduction to some basic facts about French as well as important similarities and differences between French and English.

Reading French

French is based on the same 26-letter alphabet as English, although the importance of individual letters varies. For example, the letter Q is significantly more common in French than in English, while K and W are extremely rare in French, found only in words borrowed from other languages.

Fact

The differing importance in individual letters can be seen in the fact that the French keyboard layout is called AZERTY (referring to the first six letters in the top row), as opposed to the English layout, QWERTY.

Like English, French can be very difficult in terms of pronunciation due to intricacies such as silent letters, multiple sounds for a single letter, and endless exceptions to whatever rules you manage to pin down. Therefore, the pronunciation key provided here does not explain how to read every letter combination in every situation, but rather attempts to simplify French pronunciation, to make it easier for you to get started. The key presents French letters and letter combinations, how they are represented in pronunciation guides used for that sound throughout this book, and a comparable sound in English, or in a French expression used in English.

PRONUNCIATION KEY

French Letter(s)	English Representation	Comparable English Pronunciation
A	a	"a" in father
AI	ay	"ai" in pain
AU	o	"au" in taupe
B	b	"b" in baby
C	k	"c" in can
	s	"c" in ceiling
Ç	s	"ç" in façade
CH	sh	"ch" in champagne
D	d	"d" in dad
E, EU	eu	"e" in de facto
É	ay	"é" in fiancé
È, Ê, EI	eh	"e" in bet
EAU	o	"eau" in eau de toilette
F	f	"f" in fat
G	g	"g" in gag
	zh	"g" in mirage
H		"h" in hour (silent)
I, Ï, Î	ee	"ï" in naïve
J	zh	"j" in déjà vu
K	k	"k" in kilo (rare in French)
L	l	"l" in little
M	m	"m" in mom
	(n)	(nasal vowel)
N	n	"n" in noun
	(n)	(nasal vowel)
O	o	first "o" in solo
OI	wa	"oie" in foie gras

PRONUNCIATION KEY (continued)

French Letter(s)	English Representation	Comparable English Pronunciation
OU	oo	"ou" in soup
P	p	"p" in paper
PH	f	"ph" in phone
Q	k	"q" in pique
R	r	no equivalent
S	s	"s" in sassy
SC	sk	"sc" in scold
	s	"sc" in science
T	t	"t" in tight
TH	t	"t" in tea
TI	s	"s" in silly
U	u	"oo" in food
UE	weh	"ue" in suede
UI	wee	"ui" in cuisine
V	v	"v" in verve
W	v	"v" in verve (rare in French)
X	ks	"x" in express
	gz	"x" in example
Y	y	"y" in yogurt
Z	z	"z" in zone

Ⓔ Essential

There are five different French accents (four for vowels and one for a consonant), which are very important—a missing accent is a spelling mistake, just as a missing letter would be in English.

The Letter H

H is always silent in French, but it may be silent *(H muet)* or aspirated *(H aspiré)*. These two types of the silent H act differently. The *H muet* acts like a vowel, so a word that begins with *H muet* contracts and forms liaisons just like words beginning with vowels do. In contrast, the *H aspiré* acts like a consonant, so words that begin with *H aspiré* do not allow contractions or liaisons.

Nasal Vowels

Vowels followed by M or N at the end of a word or followed by another consonant are usually nasal. A nasal vowel is a sound made by expelling air through the mouth and nose, rather than just the mouth, which can be very different from the normal pronunciation of the same vowels. Although nasal vowels also exist in English, they are a bit different, as they are only found inside a syllable, not at the end, as is common in French. For example, in the word "own," the sound just before you actually say the N is a nasal vowel: [o(n)n]. In contrast, the French word *"on"* is pronounced [o(n)]—the word ends with the nasal vowel; there is no N sound after it.

The Letter R

The French R is a classic problem for English speakers. It is similar in pronunciation to the Spanish J and the Arabic KH, if that helps you any. If not, here is a quick little exercise to help you pronounce the French R:

1. Open your mouth and close your throat (as if to keep from swallowing a mouthful of liquid).
2. Say K carefully, several times. Pay attention to where in your throat the K sound is made; henceforth, think of it as the K place.
3. Begin slowly closing your throat, until you can almost feel the K place. Your throat should be only partially constricted.
4. Tense the muscles around the K place.
5. Gently push air through your partially constricted throat. Voilà—the French R!

Practice saying Ra-Ra-Ra (where R = steps 3–5) every day.

The Letter U

The French U is also very difficult. This sound does not exist in English; the closest being the OU in soup, but that sound also exists in French. In French, the U is a separate sound and it is essential to distinguish between it and OU. To pronounce the French U, follow these steps:

1. Open your mouth and say O.
2. Draw out the O until your lips are where they would be to make a W sound.
3. Purse your lips as tightly as you can.
4. Keeping your lips pursed, say E. Voilà—the French U!

Practice saying the U with the following pairs:

tu	*tout*
vu	*vous*
lu	*loup*
su	*sous*

 Fact

French is a Romance language, although that's not why it's often called the language of love. In linguistic terms, "Romance" has nothing to do with love; it is based on the word Roman and simply means "from Latin."

Contractions

Contractions—the dropping of one or more letters and replacing them with an apostrophe—are optional in English but required in French. For example, in English you can say "I am" or "I'm"; the latter is somewhat less formal. In contrast, you cannot say "*je ai*" (I have) in French; you must make the contraction *j'ai*.

There are three main types of French contractions:

1. The words *ce, de, je, la, le, me, ne, que, se,* and *te* contract with the word that follows if it begins with a vowel or *H muet.*

    ce + est . . . .*c'est* . . . . it is
    de + histoire . . . *d'histoire* . . . . of/about history

je + habite	j'habite	I live
je le + ai	je l'ai	I have it
la + amie	l'amie	the friend
le + homme	l'homme	the man
il me + adore	il m'adore	he adores me
il ne + est pas	il n'est pas	it isn't
que + il	qu'il	that it
il se + appelle	il s'appelle	his name is
je te + aime	je t'aime	I love you

2. The prepositions *à* (to, at, in) and *de* (of, from, about) contract with the definite articles *le* and *les*, but not with *la* and *l'*:

à + le	au
à + les	aux
à + la	à la
à + l'	à l'

de + le	*du*
de + les	*des*
de + la	*de la*
de + l'	*de l'*

3. *Si + il(s)* contracts, but *si + elle(s)* does not:

si + il	*s'il*	if he/it
si + ils	*s'ils*	if they
si + elle	*si elle*	if she/it
si + elles	*si elles*	if they

Rhythm and Word Flow

Rhythm isn't really something that can be taught in a book, but it's good to know about, so that when you listen to French, you start hearing it. You've probably noticed—or at least heard others say—that the French language is very musical. The reason for this is that in French, words are not divided into stressed and unstressed syllables: all syllables are pronounced at the same intensity (volume). In addition, in French many final consonants are liaised or *enchaînés* onto the next word. The lack of stress marks, combined with liaisons and *enchaînements*, is what gives French its rhythm: all of the words flow together like music. In contrast, English words each have a stressed syllable and each sentence usually has one or two words that are stressed more than the others, which makes English sound comparatively choppy or staccato. At this point, you probably don't need to worry too much about rhythm and word flow, but you should be aware of it.

Rhythmic Groups

Instead of stressed and unstressed syllables, French sentences are divided into rhythmic groups—syntactically related words in the sentence. The last syllable of each rhythmic group is accentuated in two ways:

1. **Intonation:** The last syllable of each rhythmic group inside the sentence is pronounced at a higher pitch than the rest of the sentence, while the final rhythmic group's last syllable is pronounced at a lower pitch.

The only exception to this is questions: in this case, the last rhythmic group's final syllable is also at a high pitch.

2. **Tonic accent:** The French tonic accent is a slight elongation of the final syllable in each rhythmic group.

Enchaînement

Enchaînement is the phenomenon whereby the consonant sound at the end of a word is transfered to the beginning of the word that follows it. Take the phrase *il est* (he/it is). When you look at this phrase, you might be tempted to pronounce it [eel ay], but in fact the phrase is correctly pronounced [ee lay]—the L sound at the end of *il* is transferred onto the vowel that follows it. This is kind of like what happens when speaking quickly in English. If you ask "Would he come?" quickly, you are actually saying [woo dee kuhm]. In French, using *enchaînement* is expected.

Liaison

A liaison occurs when a normally silent consonant at the end of a word is pronounced at the beginning of the word that follows it. This is a little bit trickier than *enchaînement*, because it has to do with sounds that don't exist when the word is by itself. For example, *vous* (you) is pronounced [voo]. The S at the end is silent. However, when *vous* is followed by a word beginning with a vowel, as in the phrase *vous avez* (you have), the S must be pronounced as a Z: [voo za vay].

ⓔ *Question?*

What are some other ways to learn French pronunciation?

Pronunciation really isn't something that can be learned from a book. To speak French decently, you should take a class, find a tutor, talk to a native speaker, or at the very least, purchase some French audio tools.

True Cognates

One of the main components of language learning is vocabulary—memorizing the thousands of words that you need in order to talk about the world around you. For English speakers, one of the nice things about learning French is that there are some shortcuts you can take when learning vocabulary. For example, there are hundreds of true cognates, words that look similar in the two languages and have the same or similar meanings. These are nearly always nouns or adjectives.

True Cognates

Masculine noun	Feminine noun	Adjective
abandon	*absence*	*absent*
abdomen	*accusation*	*brave*
accent	*action*	*central*
accident	*architecture*	*certain*
agent	*automobile*	*civil*
air	*avenue*	*correct*

x

True Cognates (continued)

Masculine noun	Feminine noun	Adjective
angle	calorie	dental
animal	cassette	exact
art	cause	excellent
article	cigarette	final
budget	condition	fragile
client	description	horrible
commerce	destination	impossible
cousin	distance	long
crime	excuse	musical
danger	finance	partial
dessert	fortune	public
effort	image	simple
escalator	machine	six
fax	nation	unique
film	olive	urgent
fruit	photo	vacant
garage	prison	violet
golf	question	
guide	radio	
idiot	situation	
million		
pardon		
regret		
respect		
service		
taxi		
visa		
zoo		

Ⓔ *Fact*

There are thousands of cognates between French and English, but they are not always true. Get into the habit of checking with a dictionary or native speaker before assuming that similar words mean the same thing.

Spelling Equivalents

There are certain spelling equivalents that can help you to identify French and English cognates. That is, certain spelling patterns (usually suffixes) in one language have equivalent spelling patterns in the other language.

Spelling Equivalents

French	English	French examples	English examples
^	s	*forêt, hôpital*	forest, hospital
-ain(e)	-an	*Américain(e)*	American
-ais(e)	-ese	*Japonais(e)*	Japanese
-ance	-ence	*dépendance*	dependence
-ant	-ent	*indépendant*	independent
-çon	-sson	*leçon*	lesson
	-shion	*façon*	fashion
	-son	*maçon*	mason
é-	s-	*état, étudier*	state, study
-e	-y	*gloire*	glory
-é(e)	-ed	*épelé*	spelled
-é	-y	*qualité*	quality
-el(le)	-al	*personnel*	personal
		éternel	eternal

Spelling Equivalents (continued)

French	English	French examples	English examples
-en(ne)	-an	*Canadien(ne)*	Canadian
en + -ant	-ing	*en mangeant*	eating
		en lisant	reading
-ence	-ence	*violence*	violence
-ent	-ent	*apparent*	apparent
-er	to + verb	*épeler*	to spell
-eur	-or	*auteur*	author
	-our	*couleur*	color/colour
	-er	*employeur*	employer
-eux/euse	-ous	*nerveux*	nervous
-i	-y	*parti*	party
-i(e)	-ed, -t	*fini*	finished
-if/ive	-ive	*positif, motif*	positive, motive
-ique	-ic	*musique*	music
	-ical	*lyrique*	lyrical
-ir	to + verb	*finir*	to finish
-isation	-ization	*réalisation*	realization
	-isation		realisation
-iser	-ize	*idéaliser*	idealize
	-ise		idealise
-iste	-ist	*optimiste*	optimist/optimistic
-ment	-ly	*rapidement*	rapidly
-oire	-ory	*obligatoire*	obligatory
		mémoire	memory
-ois(e)	-ese	*Chinois(e)*	Chinese
-re	-er	*mètre*	meter/metre
	-re	*théâtre*	theater/theatre
-re	to + verb	*répondre*	to respond

Spelling Equivalents (continued)

French	English	French examples	English examples
-tion	-tion	*nation*	nation
-u(e)	-ed	*répondu*	responded

Please be aware that these are merely guidelines to spelling equivalents between French and English, not hard and fast rules.

False Cognates

Although the preceding sections can be very helpful, don't let them lull you into a false sense of security. Not all words that look alike mean the same thing. There are numerous false cognates in French and English.

False cognates are words that look alike but have different meanings. There are also a number of semi-false cognates—words that have several meanings, only some of which are similar in the two languages.

False and Semi-False Cognates

assister	to attend
attendre	to wait for
avertissement	warning
blesser	to wound
cent	one hundred
chair	flesh
chance	luck
coin	corner
collège	junior high school
commander	to order

False and Semi-False Cognates (continued)

crayon	pencil
déception	disappointment
demander	to ask, to request
déranger	to bother
douche	shower
entrée	appetizer
formidable	great
gentil	nice, kind
ignorer	to be ignorant of, to not know
librairie	bookstore
monnaie	change
occasion	opportunity
pièce	room; coin
quitter	to leave
raisin	grape
rester	to stay
réunion	meeting
sale	dirty
zone	slum; area

Ⓔ *Essential*

There are hundreds of false cognates and hundreds of true cognates. The bottom line is that you just need to be careful—if a French word looks a lot like an English one, it might mean the same thing, or it might not. Look it up in the dictionary just to be on the safe side.

Chapter 2
French Grammar Basics

Although this book provides ready-to-use lists of vocabulary and phrases for every situation, it's still a good idea for you to understand the basics of French grammar. This chapter is a greatly simplified introduction to the most important aspects of French grammar. Hopefully, these mini-lessons will help you understand how to say things in French and why you need to say them that way.

Know Your Nouns

A noun is a word that represents a thing, whether that thing is concrete (e.g., a chair, a dog) or abstract (an idea, happiness). In French, all nouns have a grammatical gender—they are either masculine or feminine. The gender of some nouns makes sense: *homme* (man) is masculine, *femme* (woman) is feminine. But for many other nouns, the gender is irrelevant or even counterintuitive: *personne* (person) is always feminine, even if the person is a man!

It is very important to learn a noun's gender along with the noun itself because articles, adjectives, and some verbs must agree with nouns; that is, they change according to the gender of the noun they modify. The best way to memorize the gender of nouns is to make your vocabulary lists with the definite or indefinite article:

un homme	man
une femme	woman

Some nouns have different meanings depending on whether they are masculine or feminine, so obviously if you want to make sure that you're talking about what you mean, you need to make sure to use the correct gender.

The Art of Articles

An article is a word used in front of a noun to indicate whether it is specific or unspecific. French articles must agree in gender and number with the nouns they modify. There are three kinds of French articles: definite, indefinite, and partitive.

Definite Articles

The French definite article, which corresponds to "the" in English, has three forms:

le	masculine/singular	*le garçon* (the boy)
la	feminine/singular	*la fille* (the girl)
les	plural	*les filles* (the girls)

And don't forget that when the noun begins with a vowel or the silent H, the definite articles *le* and *la* form a contraction:

l'ami	the friend (masculine)
l'amie	the friend (feminine)
l'homme	the man (masculine)
l'histoire	the history (feminine)

Ⓔ Fact

In French, the definite article may be used to indicate the general sense of a noun: *J'aime la glace.* (I like ice cream.) *C'est la vie!* (That's life!)

Indefinite Articles

The singular French indefinite articles correspond to "a," "an," or "one" in English. The plural corresponds to "some." There are three forms of the French indefinite article:

un	masculine/singular	*un garçon* (a boy)
une	feminine/singular	*une fille* (a girl)
des	plural	*des filles* (some girls)

In French, the indefinite article may be used to refer to just one of something: *Il y a un étudiant dans la salle.* (There is one student in the room.) When referring to a person's profession with state-of-being verbs like *être* (to be) and *devenir* (to become), the article is not used in French (although it is used in English): *Je suis professeur.* (I am a teacher.) In a negative construction, the indefinite article changes to *de*, meaning "not any": *Je n'ai pas de pommes.* (I don't have any apples.)

Partitive Articles

The partitive articles in French correspond to "some" or "any" in English. There are three forms of the French partitive article:

du	masculine/singular	*du pain* (some bread)
de la	feminine/singular	*de la bière* (some beer)
des	plural	*des haricots* (some beans)

In addition, if a singular noun starts with a vowel or a silent H, use the contraction *de l'*:

| *de l'oignon* | some onion (masculine) |
| *de l'huile* | some oil (feminine) |

The partitive article indicates an unknown or unspecified quantity of something, usually food or drink. It is often omitted in English. Here are a few examples:

Avez-vous bu du thé ?
Did you drink (some) tea?

J'ai mangé de la salade hier.
I ate (some) salad yesterday.

Nous avons des petits pois.
We have (some) peas.

After adverbs of quantity such as *beaucoup de* (a lot), *peu de* (a little), *assez de* (enough), *plus de* (more), and *moins de* (less), *de* is used instead of the partitive article:

Il y a beaucoup de problèmes.
There are a lot of problems.

J'ai moins de glace que Thierry.
I have less ice cream than Thierry.

Like the indefinite article, the partitive article changes to *de*, meaning "any," in a negative construction:

J'ai mangé de la soupe.
I ate some soup.

Je n'ai pas mangé de soupe.
I didn't eat any soup.

Ⓔ Essential

French articles are sometimes confusing for students of French, because they have to agree with the noun they modify and don't always correspond to articles in other languages. As a general rule, if you have a noun in French, there is virtually always an article in front of it, unless you use a possessive (*mon, ton,* etc.) or demonstrative (*ce, cette,* etc.) adjective.

Verbs Mean Action

A verb is the action word in a sentence. It is the word that says what happens (I walk) or describes a state of being (I am happy). All French verbs have to be conjugated or inflected—changed according to how they are used. In the English present tense, we only have a separate conjugation for the third person singular of a verb: "I want" becomes "he wants." The verb "to be" is the most complicated English verb, with three conjugations: I am, you are, he is. In other tenses and moods, English has a single form: I sang, he sang, I will go, he will go.

In stark contrast, each French verb has up to six different conjugations in each tense and mood. In most cases, French verbs are conjugated by removing the infinitive ending to find the radical or root, then adding the ending appropriate to the grammatical person, tense, and mood. These endings are different for each tense and mood, which means that each verb has a total of dozens of different forms. But don't get discouraged! There are patterns to the conjugations of most verbs.

There are a total of five elements in conjugation: number, person, voice, mood, and tense.

Number, Person, Subject Pronouns

Number and person go hand-in-hand and together indicate the grammatical person: who or what is performing the action of the verb. Number, logically enough, is divided into singular (one) and plural (more than one). As for person, there is first person (the speaker), second person (the listener), and third person (neither the speaker nor the listener). So there are two numbers and three persons, making a total of six grammatical persons, each of which has at least one subject pronoun:

	Singular	**Plural**
1st person	*je* (I)	*nous* (we)
2nd person	*tu* (you)	*vous* (you)
3rd person	*il* (he, it)	*ils* (they)
	elle (she, it)	*elles* (they, fem.)
	on (one)	

Notes

There are two words for "you" in French: *tu* and *vous*. These are not interchangeable, so it is very important to understand when and why to use each of them. Otherwise, you may inadvertantly insult someone by using the wrong "you" form.

- *Tu* is the familiar "you" form. It demonstrates a certain closeness and informality; you should use *tu* when speaking to a friend, relative, child, or pet.
- *Vous* is the formal and plural "you" form. Use *vous* when speaking to someone you don't know well, someone older than you, an authority figure, anyone to whom you wish to show respect, and anytime you are talking to two or more people.

Ⓔ *Alert!*

The importance of using the correct "you" form cannot be overstressed. There are even verbs for them: *tutoyer* means to address someone with *tu* and *vouvoyer* means to address with *vous*. As a general rule, use *vous* when traveling—it's better to show someone too much respect than not enough!

Since all nouns are either masculine or feminine, they use the third person subject pronouns that correspond to their gender. Thus *il* can refer to a male (he) or a masculine noun (it) and *elle* can refer to a female (she) or a feminine noun (it).

On is the indefinite subject pronoun. Its English equivalents can be the passive voice or indefinite subjects like "people," "we," "one," "they," or "you":

On ne fait pas ça.
That isn't done.

On est fou !
People are crazy!

On va sortir ce soir.
We're going out tonight.

Ils is used for men, male nouns, and mixed gender groups. *Elles* can only be used for a group of women and/or female nouns. In other words, the masculine pronoun is the default; the feminine pronoun can be used only when there is not a single male in the group.

Note that the pronouns *il*, *elle*, and *on* are all third person singular personal pronouns and thus take the same verb conjugation. Likewise, *ils* and *elles* both take the third person plural conjugation.

Find Your Voice

Voice refers to the relationship between the subject and verb. There are three voices in French: active (the subject performs the action), passive (the action is performed on the subject by an agent), and reflexive (the subject performs the action on itself). Active voice is the most common, followed by reflexive voice.

Get in the Mood

Mood refers to the attitude of the speaker toward the action/state of the verb—how likely or factual a statement is. The French language has three to six moods, depending on your definition. The three moods that everyone agrees on are indicative, subjunctive, and imperative, while the conditional, infinitive, and participle may or may not be considered moods by different grammarians.

- **Indicative:** The "normal" mood that indicates a fact: *J'aime lire.* (I like to read.) *Nous avons mangé.* (We ate.) The indicative is the most common mood and has the most tenses.
- **Subjunctive:** A mood that expresses subjectivity, such as doubt and unlikelihood: *Je veux que tu le fasses.* (I want you to do it.) *Il est rare que Chantal sache la réponse.* (It's rare for Chantal to know the answer.)
- **Imperative:** The mood of command. *Écris la lettre.* (Write the letter.) *Allons-y !* (Let's go!)
- **Conditional:** Describes a condition or possibility. *J'aimerais aider.* (I would like to help.) *Si tu venais avec nous, tu apprendrais beaucoup.* (If you came with us, you would learn a lot.)
- **Infinitive:** The name of the verb which can be used as a noun.
- **Participle:** The adjectival form of the verb.

Ⓔ *Fact*

The indicative, subjunctive, imperative, and conditional are known as personal moods, because they are conjugated according to the grammatical person they provide action for. The infinitive and participle are not conjugated and are thus called impersonal moods.

Making Sense of Tense

Tense refers to the verb's expression of time and completion of the verb's action or condition. The main tenses you will see covered in this book are present and past. If you want to talk about something in the future, you can nearly always get away with *aller* + verb (to be going to + verb—see Chapter 5).

Adjusting to Adjectives

An adjective is a word that modifies a noun. Adjectives can describe shape, color, size, and many other things about a noun. French adjectives are very different from English adjectives. In English, adjectives are always found in front of the noun, but the placement of French adjectives depends on the meaning of that particular adjective. The acronym BAGS can help you to memorize the majority of adjectives that are placed before the noun:

> **B**eauty
> **A**ge
> **G**ood and bad
> **S**ize

These adjectives are placed before the noun because they are considered inherent qualities of the noun. In addition, all non-descriptive adjectives are placed before the noun:

- Possessive adjectives: *mon, ma, mes* (my), *ton, ta, tes* (your), etc.

- Demonstrative adjectives: *ce, cet, cette* (this); *ces* (these)
- Interrogative adjectives: *quel, quelle, quels, quelles* (which)

All other adjectives should be placed following the noun they modify. Furthermore, French adjectives change to agree in gender and number with the nouns that they modify. This means that there can be up to four forms of each adjective: masculine singular, feminine singular, masculine plural, and feminine plural. The rules for making the majority of adjectives feminine and plural are fairly straightforward:

- Most adjectives add an E for feminine and an S for plural: *vert, verts, verte, vertes.*
- When the adjective ends in E, there is no difference between the masculine and feminine forms: *rouge, rouges.*
- When the adjective ends in S or X, there is no difference between the singular and plural masculine forms: *gris, grise, grises.*

Advantages to Adverbs

An adverb is an invariable word—that is, it does not have variant endings. An adverb may modify a verb, an adjective, or another adverb. Adverbs can provide additional information about time, manner, place, frequency, or quantity. They explain when, how, where, how often, or to what degree something is done.

The placement of French adverbs can be difficult. Whereas in English their placement is sometimes arbitrary (they may be found in front of or after the verb, or at the beginning or end of the sentence), the placement rules for French adverbs are much more strict. Here is a quick overview:

- When the adverb is modifying a verb, it is placed after the verb: *Je regarde souvent la télé le soir.* (I often watch TV in the evening.)
- When the adverb is modifying an adjective or another adverb, it is placed in front of that word: *Je suis profondément ému.* (I am deeply moved.)

🄔 *Alert!*

This chapter presents a short and very simplified introduction to French grammar. It is impossible to explain everything in a single chapter, so it's very likely that you will eventually run across things that seem to contradict what you learned here.

Preparing for Prepositions

Prepositions are the little words placed in front of nouns in order to indicate a relationship between that noun and a verb, an adjective, or another noun. Here are some common French prepositions:

à.	to, at, in
après	after
avant	before
avec.	with
chez.	at the home/office of, among
dans.	in
de	from, of, about
depuis.	since, for
en	in, on, to
pendant. . . .	during, while
pour.	for
sans.	without
sur.	on
vers	toward

Progress with Pronouns

Pronouns are words that substitute for nouns. There are more than a dozen different kinds of French pronouns, but the most important for you as a traveler are subject, direct object, indirect object, reflexive, and relative pronouns. All but relative pronouns change according to the grammatical person that they represent. You already learned about subject pronouns—which are required with all verb forms except the imperative—in the verb section. Now take a look at some other important kinds of pronouns.

Direct Object Pronouns

Just as in English, the French language has direct object pronouns, words that replace the direct object. This is so that we don't say things like "Marie was at the bank today. When I saw Marie, I smiled." It's much more natural to say "Marie was at the bank today. When I saw her, I smiled."

The direct object is the person or thing that receives the action of the verb in a sentence. To find the direct object in a sentence, ask the question "who?" or "what?" For example: I'm eating bread. What am I eating? Bread. The French direct object pronouns are as follows:

me. . . . . . me
te . . . . . . you
le . . . . . . him, it (masc)
la . . . . . . her, it (fem)
nous. . . . . us
vous. . . . . you
les. . . . . . them

Note that *me, te,* and *le/la* change to *m', t',* and *l'* in front of a vowel or silent H.

The most difficult aspect of direct object pronouns is that they go in front of the verb in French.

Je le mange.
I'm eating it.

Il la voit.
He sees her.

Je t'aime.
I love you.

Tu m'aimes.
You love me.

Indirect Object Pronouns

Indirect objects are the people or things in a sentence to/for whom/what the action of the verb occurs. I'm talking to Pierre. To whom am I talking? To Pierre (to him). Indirect object pronouns are the words that replace the indirect object. The French indirect object pronouns are:

me. . . . . . me
te. . . . . . you
lui . . . . . . him, her, it
nous. . . . . us
vous. . . . . you
leur . . . . . them

Note that *me* and *te* change to *m'* and *t'* in front of a vowel or silent H.

Like direct object pronouns, French indirect object pronouns are placed in front of the verb:

Je lui parle.
I'm talking to him.

Il leur achète des livres.
He buys books for them.

Je vous donne le pain.
I'm giving the bread to you.

Elle m'a écrit.
She wrote to me.

Reflexive Pronouns

Reflexive pronouns are used only with pronominal verbs (reflexive voice). Pronominal verbs indicate that the subject is performing the action of the verb upon him/her/itself.

Reflexive pronouns agree with the subject of the sentence. Like direct and indirect object pronouns, the reflexive pronoun is placed directly in front of the verb in all tenses except the imperative. The reflexive pronouns are:

subject pronoun	reflexive pronoun
je	*me*
tu	*te*
il, elle, on	*se*
nous	*nous*
vous	*vous*
ils, elles	*se*

Note that *me, te,* and *se* change to *m', t',* and *s'* in front of a vowel or silent H.

Sentences which need a reflexive pronoun still need a subject pronoun as well—don't let what appears to be redundancy throw you off.

Je me lève.
I'm getting up.

Il se rase.
He is shaving.

Nous nous parlons.
We're talking to each other.

Ils ne s'habillent pas.
They aren't getting dressed.

ⓔ *Essential*

When deciding between direct and indirect objects, in general, you can use the following rule: if the person or thing is preceded by a preposition, that person/thing is an indirect object. If it is not preceded by a preposition, it is a direct object.

Reflexive verbs often have to do with parts of the body or clothing. You can recognize reflexive verbs by the *se* which precedes the infinitive. Here are some common reflexive verbs:

s'asseoir	to sit down
se brosser (les cheveux, les dents)	to brush (one's hair, one's teeth)
se casser (la jambe)	to break (one's leg)
se coiffer	to fix one's hair
se coucher	to go to bed
se déshabiller	to get undressed
se doucher	to take a shower
se fâcher	to get angry
s'habiller	to get dressed
se laver (les mains, la figure)	to wash (one's hands, one's face)
se lever	to get up

se maquiller . . . . to put on makeup
se raser . . . . to shave
se regarder . . . . to look at oneself
se réveiller . . . . to wake up
se souvenir de . . . . . . to remember

Relative Pronouns

Just as in English, a French relative pronoun links a dependent/relative clause (i.e., a clause that cannot stand alone) to a main clause. *Qui* and *que* are the most important French relative pronouns for your purposes. There are no standard translations for these words; depending on context, the English equivalents are who, whom, that, or which. Note that in French, relative pronouns are required, whereas in English, they are sometimes optional.

- *Qui* replaces the subject (person or thing) in the dependent clause:

  Je cherche l'artiste. Il étudie à Paris.
  Je cherche l'artiste qui étudie à Paris.
  I'm looking for the artist (who is) studying in Paris.

  Trouvez le chat. Il habite la cave.
  Trouvez le chat qui habite la cave.
  Find the cat that lives in the basement.

- *Qui* also replaces an indirect object (person only) after a preposition:

  C'est la femme avec qui je travaille.
  That's the woman with whom I work.

  La fille à qui j'ai parlé est très sympathique.
  The girl to whom I spoke is very nice.

  L'étudiant à côté de qui je me suis assis . . .
  The student next to whom I sat . . .

- *Que* replaces the direct object (person or thing):

  J'ai acheté le livre. Ma soeur l'a écrit.
  J'ai acheté le livre que ma soeur a écrit.
  I bought the book (that) my sister wrote.

  Qui est le peintre ? Je l'ai vu aujourd'hui.
  Qui est le peintre que j'ai vu aujourd'hui ?
  Who is the painter (that) I saw today?

Ⓔ *Question?*

Why isn't *qui* always used to mean "who"?
In French, *que* and *qui* can both mean "who." The one you use depends on whether the word is replacing the subject or the direct object. Subject: *Je vois l'homme qui l'a fait.* (I see the man who did it.) Direct object: *Je vois l'homme que j'aime.* (I see the man I love.)

In the Negative

Making sentences negative in French is a bit different than in English, due to the two-part negative adverb. To make a sentence or question negative, place *ne* in front of the conjugated verb and *pas* after it. *Ne . . . pas* translates roughly as "not."

Je suis riche. Je ne suis pas riche.
I'm rich. I'm not rich.

Il veut skier. Il ne veut pas skier.
He wants to ski. He doesn't want to ski.

Vous êtes fatigué ? Vous n'êtes pas fatigué ?
Are you tired? Aren't you tired?

More negative adverbs:

ne . . . pas encore	not yet
ne . . . toujours pas	still not
ne . . . pas du tout	not at all
ne . . . plus	no more, not anymore
ne . . . jamais	never
ne . . . que	only

Il n'est pas encore prêt.
He isn't ready yet.

Je ne lui parle toujours pas.
I still don't talk to him.

Je n'aime pas du tout les épinards.
I don't like spinach at all.

Vous ne travaillez plus ?
You don't work anymore?

Nous ne voyageons jamais.
We never travel.

Il n'y a que deux chiens.
There are only two dogs.

Asking Questions

There are three simple ways to ask questions in French:

1. Put *est-ce que* at the beginning of any sentence:

   Est-ce que tu danses ?
   Do you dance?

   Est-ce que tu aimes danser ?
   Do you like to dance?

2. Add the tag *n'est-ce pas* to the end of the sentence (when you expect the answer to be yes):

   Tu danses, n'est-ce pas ?
   You dance, right?

   Tu aimes danser, n'est-ce pas ?
   You like to dance, right?

3. Raise the pitch of your voice at the end of any sentence (informal):

   Tu danses ?
   You dance?

Chapter 3
Essential French

This chapter contains some of the most important French vocabulary for travelers. It includes essential phrases like "Do you speak English?" and "I don't understand" as well as polite phrases, yes/no, numbers, calendar vocabulary, and instructions for telling time.

Survival French

Take a look at the following French phrases—they might come in handy as you begin communicating:

I speak a little French.
Je parle un peu français.
zheu parl uh(n) peu fra(n) seh

Do you speak English?
Parlez-vous anglais ?
par lay voo a(n) gleh

What does . . . mean?
Que veut-dire . . . ?
keu veu deer

How do you say . . . in French?
Comment dit-on . . . en français ?
kuh ma(n) dee to(n) . . . a(n) fra(n) seh

Repeat, please.
Répétez, s'il vous plaît.
ray pay tay seel voo play

Ⓔ *Essential*

Try to speak as much French as you can before falling back on "Do you speak English?" The French will appreciate the effort you make, and the practice will make it increasingly easier for you to use your French with the next person you encounter.

More slowly. One more time.
Plus lentement. Encore une fois.
plu la(n) teu ma(n); a(n) kuhr oon fwa

I don't understand.
Je ne comprends pas.
zheu neu ko(n) pra(n) pa

I don't know. What?
Je ne sais pas. Comment ?
zheu neu say pa; kuh ma(n)

Language Basics

The following vocabulary is about the most basic there is—yes, no, and, or, and the WH questions.

yes	. . .	*oui*
		wee
no	. . . .	*non*
		no(n)
yes	. . .	*si*
		see
OK	. . .	*d'accord*
		da kuhr
and	. . .	*et*
		ay
or	. . . .	*ou*
		oo
who	. . .	*qui*
		kee

what . . *quoi*
　　　　kwa

when . . *quand*
　　　　ka(n)

where . . *où*
　　　　oo

why . . . *pourquoi*
　　　　poor kwa

how . . . *comment*
　　　　kuh ma(n)

Ⓔ *Fact*

Si is used when responding affirmatively to a negative question or statement. Compare the following: *Tu viens ? Oui.* (Are you coming? Yes.) *Tu ne viens pas ? Si.* (Aren't you coming? Yes, I am.)

Be Polite

Being polite when traveling is an absolute must. If you don't have time to learn much before you leave, at least know how to say "please" and "thank you."

please . . . . *s'il vous plaît*
　　　　　　　　　seel voo pleh
please . . . . *veuillez*
　　　　　　　　　(in front of a verb; very formal)
　　　　　　　　　veu yay

thank you . . . . *merci*
    mehr see

thank you very much . . . . *merci beaucoup*
    mehr see bo koo

thank you so much . . . . . *mille fois merci*
    meel fwa mehr see

you're welcome . . . . *de rien*
    deu ryeh(n)

it was my pleasure . . . . . . *je vous en prie*
    zheu voo za(n) pree

don't mention it . . . . *il n'y a pas de quoi*
    eel nya pa deu kwa

pardon me . . . . *pardon*
    par do(n)

excuse me . . . . *excusez-moi*
    eh sku zay mwa

I'm sorry. . . . . *je suis désolé(e)*
    zheu swee day zuh lay

bless you (after a sneeze) . . *à vos souhaits*
    a vo sweh

cheers . . . . *à votre santé*
    a vuh treu sa(n) tay

Titles

Sir, Mr. . . . . *Monsieur*
    meu syeu

Ma'am, Mrs. . . . . *Madame*
    ma dam

Miss . . . . *Mademoiselle*
    ma deu mwa zel

I'm sorry to disturb you
Excusez-moi de vous déranger
eh sku zay mwa deu voo day ra(n) zhay

Enjoy your meal!
Bon appétit !
bo na pay tee

 Alert!

> If you approach someone to ask for help, the phrase
> *Excusez-moi de vous déranger* is essential. *Excusez-moi*
> and *pardon* should be used only when you are not going
> to continue talking to that person; e.g., when you bump
> into someone or when you need to get past someone.

Learning to Count Again

Remember learning how to count as a child? Now you get
to do it again in French!

1.	*un*	uh(n)
2	*deux*	deu
3	*trois*	trwa
4.	*quatre*	katr
5	*cinq*	seh(n)k
6	*six*	sees

7.........	*sept*	seht
8	*huit*	weet
9	*neuf*	neuf
10........	*dix*	dees
11........	*onze*	o(n)z
12........	*douze*	dooz
13........	*treize*	trehz
14........	*quatorze*	ka torz
15........	*quinze*	keh(n)z
16........	*seize*	sehz
17........	*dix-sept*	dee seht
18........	*dix-huit*	dee zweet
19........	*dix-neuf*	deez neuf
20	*vingt*	veh(n)
21........	*vingt et un*	veh(n) tay uh(n)
22.......	*vingt-deux*	veh(n) deu
23	*vingt-trois*	veh(n) trwa
(etc.)		
30	*trente*	tra(n)t
31........	*trente et un*	tra(n) tay uh(n)

32 . . . . *trente-deux*	tra(n)t deu
(etc.)	
40. . . . . *quarante*	ka ra(n)t
50 . . . . *cinquante*	seh(n) ka(n)t
60 . . . . *soixante*	swa sa(n)

For 20 through 69, counting is almost just like in English: the tens word (*vingt*, *trente*, *quarante*, etc.) followed by the ones word (*un*, *deux*, *trois*). The only difference is that for 21, 31, etc., the word "et" is introduced between the tens word and one: *vingt-et-un, trente-et-un, quarante-et-un*, etc.

Then it gets trickier. In French, 70 is literally "sixty-ten." 71 is *soixante et onze* (sixty and eleven), 72 is *soixante-douze* (sixty-twelve), and so on:

70. . . . . *soixante-dix*	swa sa(n)t dees
71. . . . . *soixante et onze*	swa sa(n) tay o(n)z
72. . . . . *soixante-douze*	swa sa(n)t dooz
73. . . . . *soixante-treize*	swa sa(n)t trehz
74. . . . . *soixante-quatorze*	swa sa(n)t ka tuhrz

80 is literally four-twenties (think four-score), 81 is four-twenty-one, and so on, all the way up to 90. 90 is four-twenty-ten, 91 is four-twenty-eleven, etc.

Ⓔ *Essential*

In Belgium and Switzerland, you don't need to do quite so much math when counting to a hundred. Seventy is *septante* and ninety is *nonante* to French speakers in both countries. As for 80, Belgians do say *quatre-vingts*, but the Swiss say *huitante*.

80	*quatre-vingts*	ka treu veh(n)
81	*quatre-vingt-un*	ka treu veh(n) tuh(n)
82	*quatre-vingt-deux*	ka treu veh(n) deu
90	*quatre-vingt-dix*	ka treu veh(n) dees
91	*quatre-vingt-onze*	ka treu veh(n) to(n)z
(etc.)		
100.	*cent*	sa(n)
200	*deux cents*	deu sa(n)
1,000	*mille*	meel
2,000.	*deux mille*	deu meel
1,000,000. . .	*un million*	uh(n) mee lyo(n)

2,000,000	*deux millions*	deu mee lyo(n)
a billion	*un milliard*	uh(n) mee lyar
trillion	*un billion*	uh(n) bee lyo(n)

Note that *un billion* is a false cognate, as mentioned in Chapter 1.

Telling Time

French doesn't have words for "a.m." and "p.m." In theory, you can use *du matin* for a.m., *de l'après-midi* from noon until 6 p.m., and *du soir* from 6 p.m. until midnight, but that is not common. Instead, time is usually expressed on a 24-hour clock. Thus 3 p.m. would be translated as *quinze heures* or *15h*.

What time is it? It's . . .
Quelle heure est-il ? Il est . . .
keh leur ay teel; ee lay

one o'clock	*une heure*
	u neur
two o'clock	*deux heures*
	deu zeur
3:30	*trois heures trente/et demie*
	trwa zeur tra(n)t/ay deu mee
4:15	*quatre heures et quart*
	ka treur ay kar

4:45. . . . . . *cinq heures moins le quart*
seh(n) keur mwa(n) leu kar

5:10. . . . . . *cinq heures dix*
seh(n) keur dees

6:50 . . . . . *six heures cinquante/sept heures moins dix*
see zeur seh(n) ka(n)s/eh teur mwa(n) dees

7 a.m. . . . . *sept heures du matin*
seh teur du ma teh(n)

3 p.m. . . . . *trois heures de l'après-midi/quinze heures*
trwa zeur deu la preh mee dee/keh(n) zeur

6 p.m. . . . . *six heures du soir/dix-huit heures*
see zeur du swar/dee zwee teur

noon. . . . . . *midi*
mee dee

midnight. . . *minuit*
mee nwee

Ⓔ *Fact*

There's one other way to say 4:15: *quatre heures quinze,*
pronounced "ka treur keh(n)z." Furthermore, there are
two additional ways to say 4:45: *cinq heures moins quinze,*
pronounced "seh(n) keur mwa(n) keh(n)z," and *quatre
heures quarante-cinq,* pronounced "ka treur ka ra(n)t
seh(n)k."

The Calendar

The French calendar isn't too difficult, but there are two things to be aware of: the French week starts on Monday, and days and months are not capitalized in French.

Days of the Week

Monday	*lundi*	luh(n) dee
Tuesday	*mardi*	mar dee
Wednesday	*mercredi*	mehr kreu dee
Thursday	*jeudi*	zheu dee
Friday	*vendredi*	va(n) dreu dee
Saturday	*samedi*	sam dee
Sunday	*dimanche*	dee ma(n)sh

Months of the Year

January	*janvier*	zha(n) vyay
February	*février*	fay vree ay
March	*mars*	mars
April	*avril*	a vreel
May	*mai*	may
June	*juin*	zhweh(n)
July	*juillet*	zhwee yay
August	*août*	oot
September	*septembre*	sehp ta(n) br
October	*octobre*	uhk tuh br
November	*novembre*	nuh va(n) br
December	*décembre*	day sa(n) br

Seasons

spring	*printemps*	preh(n) ta(n)
summer	*été*	ay tay
autumn	*automne*	oh tuhn
winter	*hiver*	ee vehr

Chapter 4
Meeting People

Wherever you go, it's a good idea to know how to greet people and exchange pleasantries in the local language. Aside from showing respect for the language and culture of that country, being able to chat with the people you meet will make your trip more enjoyable and less frustrating, for yourself as well as the locals.

Greetings

Whether going into a store, buying bread, or asking for directions in France, try to make a point of saying hello and good-bye to the employees and other people you talk to. You'll notice that French people do the same—it's common courtesy.

Greetings

Hello.	*Bonjour*	bo(n) zhoor
Hi	*Salut*	sa lu
Good evening. . . .	*Bonsoir*	bo(n) swar

Leavetakings

Bye.	*Salut*
	sa lu
Good-bye	*Au revoir*
	o reu vwar
Good night	*Bonne nuit*
	buhn nwee
See you soon	*À bientôt, à tout à l'heure*
	a byeh(n) to; a too ta leur
See you tomorrow .	*À demain*
	a deu meh(n)
Until next time . . .	*À la prochaine*
	a la pruh shen
Farewell	*Adieu*
	a dyeu

There are several different ways of saying "How are you?"

Ça va ?
sa va

Comment ça va ?
kuh ma(n) sa va

Comment allez-vous ?
kuh ma(n) ta lay voo

Comment vas-tu ?
kuh ma(n) va tu

You can also ask the following questions:

How's it going?
Ça roule ? Ça bouge ?
sa rool; sa boozh

What's up?
Quoi de neuf ?
kwa deu neuf

Appropriate Responses

Fine	*Ça va*	sa va
I'm doing well. .	*Ça va bien*	sa va byeh(n)
Not well	*Ça va mal*	sa va mal
So-so.	*Comme ci, comme ça*	kum see kum sa

Appropriate Responses (continued)

I'm fine . . . . *Je vais bien*
zheu vay byeh(n)

Not much . . . . . . *Pas grand chose*
pa gra(n) shoz

Not bad . . . . *Pas mal*
pa mal

Nothing new . . . . *Rien de nouveau*
ryeh(n) deu noo vo

 Alert!

> The version of "How are you?" that you should use
> depends mainly on whether you use *tu* or *vous* with
> the person. *Ça va* can be used with anyone, whereas *ça
> roule, ça bouge,* and *quoi de neuf* are informal and should
> be used only with close friends.

Introductions

When meeting people for the first time, there are just a
couple of formulas that you need to be aware of.

What's your name? (formal)
Comment vous appelez-vous ?
kuh ma(n) voo za play voo

What's your name? (informal)
Comment tu t'appelles ?
kuh ma(n) tu ta pehl

I'd like to introduce . . . (formal)
Je vous présente . . .
zheu voo pray za(n)t

I'd like to introduce . . . (informal)
Je te présente . . .
zheu teu pray za(n)t

His name is . . .
Il s'appelle . . .
eel sa pehl

Her name is . . .
Elle s'appelle . . .
ehl sa pehl

My name is . . .
Je m'appelle . . .
zheu ma pel

Pleased to meet you.
Enchanté.
a(n) sha(n) tay

The Verb Avoir

Avoir means "to have" and is one of the most common French verbs:

> I have a problem.
> *J'ai un problème.*
> zhay uh(n) pruh blehm

> He has three brothers.
> *Il a trois frères.*
> ee la trwa frehr

Avoir is used in a number of idiomatic expressions, many of which are translated by "to be" in English:

to be . . . years old	*avoir . . . ans*
	a vwar . . . a(n)
to be afraid of.	*avoir peur de*
	a vwar peur deu
to be ashamed	*avoir honte*
	a vwar o(n)t
to be cold	*avoir froid*
	a vwar frwa
to be hot.	*avoir chaud*
	a vwar sho
to be hungry	*avoir faim*
	a vwar feh(n)
to be lucky	*avoir de la chance*
	a vwar deu la sha(n)s

to be right	*avoir raison*
	a vwar reh zo(n)
to be sick to	*avoir mal au cœur*
one's stomach	a vwar ma lo keur
to be sleepy	*avoir sommeil*
	a vwar suh may
to be thirsty	*avoir soif*
	a vwar swaf
to be wrong	*avoir tort*
	a vwar tor
to have a headache	*avoir mal à la tête*
	a vwar ma la la tet
to have a stomachache . .	*avoir mal à l'estomac*
	a vwar ma la leh stuh ma
to intend to	*avoir l'intention de*
	a vwar leh(n) ta(n) syo(n) deu
to look . . . (adjective) . . .	*avoir l'air* + adjective
	a vwar lehr
to look like a . . . (noun) . .	*avoir l'air de* + noun
	a vwar lehr deu
to need	*avoir besoin de*
	a vwar beu zweh(n) deu
to want	*avoir envie de*
	a vwar a(n) vee deu

How old are you? I'm thirty (years old).
Quel âge avez-vous / as-tu ? J'ai 30 ans.
keh lazh a vay voo / a tu; zhay tra(n) ta(n)

Ⓔ *Question?*

Are you wondering how to know whether *avoir* means "to have" or "to be"?
The only answer is memorization—you just have to learn the list of idiomatic expressions that use *avoir*.

The verb conjugations for *avoir* are irregular:

	Past	Present	Future
j'	*avais* [a veh]	*ai* [ay]	*aurai* [o ray]
tu	*avais* [a veh]	*as* [a]	*auras* [o ra]
il	*avait* [a veh]	*a* [a]	*aura* [o ra]
nous	*avions* [a vyo(n)]	*avons* [a vo(n)]	*aurons* [o ro(n)]
vous	*aviez* [a vyay]	*avez* [a vay]	*aurez* [o ray]
ils	*avaient* [a vay]	*ont* [o(n)]	*auront* [o ro(n)]

Nationalities and Languages

Meeting people from other countries and with different native languages is pretty much a given when you travel, and talking about where you are from is a good way to break the ice as well as an interesting way to test your knowledge of geography. The following list includes nationality adjectives in the masculine form; see Chapter 2 for an explanation of how to add feminine endings.

African. . . . . *africain*
a free keh(n)

Algerian . . . . *algérien*
al zhay ryeh(n)

(East) Asian. . . . . *asiatique*
a zee a teek

Australian . . . . . . *australien*
o stra lyeh(n)

Belgian . . . . *belge*
belzh

Brazilian. . . . . . . *brésilien*
bray zee lyeh(n)

Canadian . . . . . . *canadien*
ka na dyeh(n)

Chinese . . . . *chinois*
shee nwa

Dutch . . . . *néerlandais*
nay eur la(n) deh

Egyptian. . . . . . . *égyptien*
ay zheep syeh(n)

English . . . . *anglais*
a(n) gleh

European . . . . . . *européen*
eu ruh pay eh(n)

French. . . . . *français*
fra(n) seh

German . . . . *allemand*
a leu ma(n)

Indian . . . . *indien*
eh(n) dyeh(n)

Irish . . . . *irlandais*
eer la(n) deh

Italian . . . . *italien*
ee ta lyeh(n)

Japanese . . . . . . *japonais*
zha poh neh

Mexican. . . . . . . *mexicain*
meh ksee keh(n)

Moroccan . . . . . . *marocain*
ma roh keh(n)

Polish . . . . *polonais*
poh loh neh

Portuguese . . . . . *portugais*
pohr tu geh

Russian . . . . *russe*
rus

Senegalese . . . . . *sénégalais*
say nay ga leh

Spanish . . . . *espagnol*
eh spa nyohl

Swiss. . . . . *suisse*
swees

Ⓔ *Essential*

When these words are used as nationality adjectives, they don't need to be capitalized. However, they do need to be capitalized when used as nouns: *J'ai parlé avec un Espagnol.* (I spoke to a Spaniard.)

The Verb Être

The French verb *être* means "to be":

> I am a French teacher.
> *Je suis professeur de français.*
> zheu swee pruh feu seur deu fra(n) seh

> Are you ready?
> *Es-tu prêt ?*
> ay tu preh

Être is used with adjectives, nouns, and adverbs to describe the current or permanent state of someone or something:

> He is handsome.
> *Il est beau.*
> ee lay bo

> I'm in Paris.
> *Je suis à Paris.*
> zheu swee za pa ree

> We are French.
> *Nous sommes français.*
> noo suhm fra(n) seh

> He's over there.
> *Il est là-bas.*
> ee lay la ba

Être is an irregular verb:

	Past	Present	Future
je (j')	étais [ay teh]	suis [swee]	serai [seu ray]
tu	étais [ay teh]	es [ay]	seras [seu ra]
il	était [ay teh]	est [ay]	sera [seu ra]
nous	étions [ay tyo(n)]	sommes [suhm]	serons [seu ro(n)]
vous	étiez [ay tyay]	êtes [eht]	serez [seu ray]
ils	étaient [ay tay]	sont [so(n)]	seront [seu ro(n)]

As noted earlier, there are a number of expressions with "to be" in English which use *avoir* rather than *être*.

Family Members

Talking about family is another interesting way to share information about yourself at the same time that you get to know other people.

aunt . . . . *une tante*
ta(n)t

brother . . . . *un frère*
frehr

cousin (female). . . *une cousine*
koo zeen

cousin (male). . . . *un cousin*
koo zeh(n)

daughter. . . . . . . *une fille*
feey

father	*un père* pehr
granddaughter . . .	*une petite-fille* peu teet feey
grandfather	*un grand-père* gra(n) pehr
grandmother	*une grand-mère* gra(n) mehr
grandson	*un petit-fils* peu tee fees
husband	*un mari* ma ree
mother.	*une mère* mehr
nephew	*un neveu* neu veu
niece.	*une nièce* nyehs
sister.	*une sœur* seur
son.	*un fils* fees
uncle.	*un oncle* o(n)kl
wife	*une femme* fam

Chapter 5
Airports and Hotels

Now that you know the basic formulas for meeting people and being polite, it's time to figure out how to get where you're going and where to stay. This chapter deals with the aiport and hotel vocabulary which will help you make reservations, buy your ticket, negotiate the airport, get on the plane, go through customs, and deal with the hotel.

The Verb Vouloir

The French verb *vouloir* means "to want":

I want to dance with you.
Je veux danser avec toi.
zheu veu da(n) say a vehk twa

Do you want to speak?
Voulez-vous parler ?
voo lay voo par lay

Vouloir is an irregular French verb, and its most important tenses are the present and past.

	Past	Present
je	*voulais* [voo leh]	*veux* [veu]
tu	*voulais* [voo leh]	*veux* [veu]
il	*voulait* [voo leh]	*veut* [veu]
nous	*voulions* [voo lyo(n)]	*voulons* [voo lo(n)]
vous	*vouliez* [voo lyay]	*voulez* [voo lay]
ils	*voulaient* [voo lay]	*veulent* [veul]

The future conjugation of *vouloir* isn't necessary, as you are unlikely to need to say "I will want." However, there are two additional conjugations of *vouloir* which you will find helpful when making requests: *voudrais* (would like) and *veuillez,* the *vous* form of the imperative, used to express a very polite request:

I'd like a ticket.
Je voudrais un billet.
zheu voo dreh uh(n) bee yay

I'd like to leave tomorrow.
Je voudrais partir demain.
zheu voo dreh par teer deu meh(n)

Please (be so kind as to) excuse me.
Veuillez m'excuser.
veu yay mehk sku zay

Please sit down.
Veuillez vous asseoir.
veu yay voo za swar

The Verb Aller

Another essential verb for travelers is *aller*, which means "to go" and is used just like its English equivalent:

I'm going to Paris.
Je vais à Paris.
zheu veh a pa ree

He's going with us.
Il va avec nous.
eel va a vek noo

 **Essential**

Remember that *je* changes to *j'* in front of a vowel, so you would say *je suis allé* and *je vais*, but *j'irai*.

Past	Present	Future
je (j')		
suis allé [swee za lay]	*vais* [vay]	*irai* [ee ray]
tu		
es allé [ayz a lay]	*vas* [va]	*iras* [ee ra]
il		
est allé [ay ta lay]	*va* [va]	*ira* [ee ra]
nous		
sommes allés [suhm za lay]	*allons* [a lo(n)]	*irons* [ee ro(n)]
vous		
êtes allé(s) [ehtz a lay]	*allez* [a lay]	*irez* [ee ray]
ils		
sont allés [so(n) ta lay]	*vont* [vo(n)]	*iront* [ee ro(n)]

As in English, the verb *aller* can be used to express the near future, usually translated as "going to." It is formed by conjugating *aller* and following it with the infinitive of the action that is about to occur:

I'm going to study.
Je vais étudier.
zheu vayz eh too dee eh

They are going to eat in 5 minutes.
Ils vont manger dans 5 minutes.
eel voh(n) mahn zheh da(n) sank meen oot

Airport and Flight Vocabulary

Armed with verb conjugations for making requests and talking about what you're going to do, you're now ready to make your reservation, buy your ticket, and get on the plane. Here are the French phrases you'll need.

People, Places, and Things

airplane	*un avion*
	a vyo(n)
airport	*un aéroport*
	a ay ruh por
baggage	*les bagages*
	ba gazh
boarding pass	*la carte d'embarquement*
	kart da(n) bar keu ma(n)
carry-on luggage	*les bagages à main*
	ba gazh a meh(n)
cart	*un chariot*
	sha ryo
checked luggage	*les bagages enregistrés*
	ba gazh a(n) reu zhee stray
check-in desk	*l'enregistrement*
	a(n) reu zhee streu ma(n)
departures	*les départs*
	day par
duty-free shop	*une boutique hors taxes*
	boo teek ohr taks
early	*en avance*
	a(n) na vans
late	*en retard*
	a(n) reu tar
passenger	*un passager*
	pa sa zhay

People, Places, and Things (continued)

passport	*un passeport*
	pas por
pilot	*le pilote*
	pee loht
security check	*le contrôle de sécurité*
	ko(n) trol deu say ku ree tay
shuttle	*une navette*
	na veht
steward	*un steward*
	steu art
stewardess	*une hôtesse de l'air*
	o tehs deu lehr
visa	*un visa*
	vee za

Ticket Information

airline	*une compagnie aérienne*
	ko(n) pa nyee a ay ryehn
economy (coach) class	*la classe touriste*
	klas too reest
first class	*la première classe*
	preu myehr klas
flight	*un vol*
	vohl
gate	*une porte*
	pohrt
one-way ticket	*un billet aller*
	bee yay a lay
plane ticket	*un billet d'avion*
	bee yay da vyo(n)

Ticket Information (continued)

round-trip ticket . . . . . *un billet aller-retour*
bee yay a lay reu toor

stopover . . . . *une escale*
eh skal

terminal . . . . *une aérogare*
a ay roh gar

Travel Verbs

to board . . . . *embarquer*
a(n) bar kay

to buy a ticket. . . . . . . *acheter un billet*
a sheu tay uh(n) bee yay

to check bags. . . . . . . *enregistrer (les bagages)*
a(n) reu zhee stray

to make a reservation . . *faire une réservation*
fehr oon ray zehr va syo(n)

to sit down . . . . *s'asseoir*
sa swar

to take off . . . . *décoller*
day koh lay

 Fact

These verbs are in the infinitive and can be directly preceded by conjugations of the other verbs you have learned. For example, *Je voudrais acheter un billet.* (I'd like to buy a ticket.) *Nous allons embarquer.* (We're going to board.)

Baggage Claim, Immigration, and Customs

Once you've arrived at your destination, you need to collect your luggage and go through immigration and customs. Here is the vocabulary you may need.

Arrivals and Baggage

to land	*atterrir*
	a tay reer
arrivals	*les arrivées*
	a ree vay
baggage claim	*la réception des bagages*
	ray sehp syo(n) day ba gazh

My luggage is missing.
Mes bagages sont égarés.
may ba gazh so(n) tay ga ray

Immigration and Customs

immigration	*l'immigration*
	ee mee gra syo(n)
immigration form . . .	*le formulaire d'immigration*
	fohr moo lehr dee mee gra syo(n)
last name	*le nom de famille*
	no(n) deu fa meey
first name	*le prénom*
	pray no(n)
customs	*la douane*
	dwan
nothing to declare . . .	*rien à déclarer*
	ryeh na day kla ray

customs declaration form
le formulaire de douane
fuhr moo lehr deu dwan

Here's my passport.
Voici mon passeport.
vwa see mo(n) pas pohr

I have a visa.
J'ai un visa.
zhay uh(n) vee za.

I don't have a visa.
Je n'ai pas de visa.
zheu nay pa deu vee za

I would like to declare . . . .
Je voudrais déclarer . . .
zheu voo dreh day kla ray

Get a Room!

You made it! After your flight and airport negotiations, you're probably ready to take a nap before going out to explore the town. Here are some words and phrases for getting the accommodations you want.

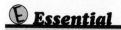 **Essential**

In some inexpensive French hotels, the bathroom is often down the hall. If you want a toilet/sink/shower in your room, you need to make that clear when reserving your room.

I would like a room for/with . . .
Je voudrais une chambre pour/avec . . .
zheu voo dreh oon sha(n)br poor/a vehk

one night.	*une nuit*	
	oon nwee	
two nights	*deux nuits*	
	deu nwee	
one person.	*une personne*	
	oon pehr sohn	
two people.	*deux personnes*	
	deu pehr sohn	
two beds	*deux lits*	
	deu lee	
a double bed	*un grand lit*	
	u(n) gra(n) lee	
a shower in the room .	*une douche dans la chambre*	
	oon doosh da(n) la sha(n)br	
a bathtub	*une baignoire*	
	oon beh nwar	
a toilet	*des toilettes*	
	day twa leht	
a television	*une télévision*	
	oon tay lay vee zyo(n)	
a telephone	*un téléphone*	
	u(n) tay lay fuhn	
air conditioning	*la climatisation*	
	la klee ma tee zah syo(n)	

Do you have . . . ? Is there . . . ?
Avez-vous . . . ? Est-ce qu'il y a . . . ?
a vay voo; es keel ee a

elevator	*un ascenseur*
	u na sa(n) seur
laundry service	*un service de lessive*
	u(n) sehr vees deu lay seev
hairdresser/barber . . .	*un coiffeur*
	u(n) kwa feur
parking lot/garage . . .	*un parking*
	u(n) par keeng
restaurant	*un restaurant*
	u(n) reh sto ra(n)
pool	*une piscine*
	oon pee seen

At the Hotel

You're almost there—you just need to know the vocabulary to get around the hotel, pay the bill, and request a wake-up call.

hotel	*l'hôtel*
	o tehl
accommodations . . .	*le logement*
	luhzh ma(n)
no vacancy	*complet*
	co(n) pleh

1st floor (US), ground floor (UK) . . .	*le rez-de-chaussée* ray deu sho say
2nd floor (US), 1st floor (UK)	*le premier étage* preu myay ay tazh
hallway.	*le couloir* koo lwar
room.	*la chambre* sha(n)br
door	*la porte* port
window	*la fenêtre* feu nehtr
bed	*le lit* lee
pillow	*l'oreiller* o ray ay
sofa	*le canapé* ka na pay
dresser.	*la commode* kuh muhd
lamp.	*la lampe* la(n)p
bathroom	*la salle de bains* sal deu beh(n)
lavatory	*les toilettes, les W.-C.* twa leht; leh vay say
towel.	*la serviette* sehr vyeht

elevator . . . . *l'ascenseur*
sa(n) seur

laundry service . . . . . *le service de blanchisserie*
seur vees deu bla(n) shees er ee

hairdresser/barber . . . *le coiffeur*
kwa feur

parking lot/garage . . . *le parking*
par keeng

restaurant . . . . *le restaurant*
reh sto ra(n)

pool . . . . *la piscine*
pee seen

I would like a wake-up call at 8 A.M.
Je voudrais être réveillé à huit heures.
zheu voo dreh eht ray vay ay a weet eur

What is the check-out time?
Il faut libérer la chambre à quelle heure ?
eel fo lee bay ray la sha(n)br a kel leur

Paying Your Way
How much is it?
C'est combien ?
say co(n) bye(n)

I would like to pay my bill.
Je voudrais régler mon compte.
zheu voo dreh ray glay mo(n) co(n)t

The bill is incorrect.
L'addition n'est pas correcte.
la dee syo(n) nay pa kuh rehkt

I would like to pay . . .
Je voudrais payer . . .
zheu voo dreh pay ay

in cash.	*en espèces*
	a(n) eh spehs
with traveler's checks .	*avec des chèques de voyage*
	a vehk day shehk deu vwa yazh
with a credit card	*avec une carte de credit*
	a veh koon kart deu kray dee

 Alert!

Be sure to ask ahead of time if the hotel takes credit cards or traveler's checks. Small, family-run hotels and B&Bs might only accept cash.

Chapter 6
Getting Around Town

Whether you're renting your own car or planning to use public transportation, you'll need some special vocabulary. This chapter includes the French terms for various types of transportation as well as helpful phrases related to asking for directions and renting a car.

Asking for Directions

Sometimes it's fun just to wander aimlessly and discover all kinds of hidden treasures. If you're in a hurry, though, there's no shame in asking for directions.

Where is . . . ? It's . . .
Où se trouve . . . ? C'est . . .
oo seu troov; say

left	*à gauche*
	a gosh
right	*à droite*
	a drwat
straight (ahead) . . .	*tout droit*
	too drwa
next to.	*à côté de*
	a ko tay deu
in front of	*devant*
	deu va(n)
in back of	*derrière*
	deh ree air
up	*en haut*
	a(n) ho
down	*en bas*
	a(n) ba
near (to).	*près (de)*
	preh deu
far (from)	*loin (de)*
	lwa(n) deu

north.	*nord*	
	nohr	
south.	*sud*	
	sood	
east	*est*	
	ehst	
west	*ouest*	
	oo west	

Alert!

When asking for directions, be sure to incorporate the politeness, basic, and survival French vocabulary from Chapter 3.

Places to Go

How can you ask for directions if you don't know how to say the name of the place you're looking for? Here's some vocabulary to help you out.

bank	*la banque*	
	ba(n)k	
church.	*l'église*	
	ay gleez	
currency exchange. .	*le bureau de change*	
	boo ro deu sha(n)zh	
hospital	*l'hôpital*	
	o pee tal	

hotel	*l'hôtel*
	o tehl
movie theater	*le cinéma*
	see nay ma
museum	*le musée*
	moo zay
park	*le parc*
	park
police station	*le commissariat*
	ko mee sa rya
post office	*la poste*
	pohst
restaurant	*le restaurant*
	reh sto ra(n)
school	*l'école*
	ay kohl
theater	*le théâtre*
	tay ahtr

Other places you might like to go, including stores and other businesses, are covered in Chapter 8.

Ⓔ Essential

The French subway system is extremely logical and easy to use—at least once you understand it. If you'll be using the Parisian subway, be sure to obtain a copy of *Paris Pratique* at any newsstand. It includes a map of the *métro*, an index of street names with page references, and detailed street maps of the entire city.

Types of Transportation

The method of transportation you plan on using will determine which vocabulary is most useful to you, so figure that out first.

transportation	*le transport*
	tra(n) spohr
car	*la voiture*
	vwa toor
taxi.	*le taxi*
	ta ksee
taxi stand	*la station de taxi*
	sta syo(n) deu ta ksee
train	*le train*
	tra(n)
train platform.	*le quai*
	kay
train station.	*la gare*
	gar
bus.	*l'autobus*
	o to boos
bus stop	*l'arrêt du bus*
	a reh doo boos
bus station	*la gare routière*
	gar roo tyair
subway.	*le métro*
	may tro
subway station	*la gare de métro*
	gar deu may tro

bike . . . . *un vélo*
                       vay lo

moped. . . . . *une mobylette*
                       mo bee leht

boat . . . . *un bateau*
                       ba to

Renting a Car

If you're staying in a large city like Paris or going from one city to another, public transportation and trains are perfect. On the other hand, if you plan to visit numerous cities and/or the countryside, renting a car can be just the thing.

I'd like to rent a car.
Je voudrais louer une voiture.
zheu voo dreh loo ay oon vwa toor

automatic . . . . *avec transmission automatique*
                        a vehk tra(n) smee syo(n)
                            o to ma teek

economy car . . . . . *économie*
                       ay kuh noh mee

compact car . . . . . *compacte*
                       ko(n) pakt

mid-size car. . . . . . *intermédiaire*
                        e(n) tehr may dyehr

luxury car . . . . *de luxe*
                         deu looks

convertible . . . . . . *décapotable*
                        day ka poh tabl

4x4 . . . . *un quatre-quatre*
kat katr

truck . . . . *un camion*
ka myo(n)

How much will it cost?
C'est combien ?
say ko(n) bye(n)

Do I have to pay by the kilometer?
Dois-je payer au kilomètre ?
dwa zheu pay ay o kee luh metr

Is insurance included?
L'assurance est-elle comprise ?
la su ra(s) ay tehl ko(n) preez

I'd like to pay by credit card.
Je voudrais payer par carte de crédit.
zheu voo dreh pay ay par kart deu cray dee

Where can I pick up the car?
Où puis-je prendre la voiture ?
oo pwee zheu pra(n)dr la vwa toor

When do I have to return it?
Quand dois-je la rendre ?
ka(n) dwa zheu la ra(n)dr

Can I return it to Lyon/Nice?
Puis-je la rendre à Lyon/Nice ?
pwee zheu la ra(n)dr a lyo(n)/nees

ⓔ Alert!

Cars in Europe usually have manual transmissions. If you can't drive a stick-shift, be sure to do some calling around before you leave to find a rental company that offers cars with automatic transmission.

Car and Driver

There's some vocabulary that will come in handy while you're driving, but you should probably ask your co-pilot to read it to you when you're actually on the road.

brake lights	*les feux de stop*
	feu deu stuhp
brakes	*les freins*
	freh(n)
broken-down	*en panne*
	a(n) pan
driver	*un conducteur*
	ko(n) dook teur
gas, petrol	*de l'essence (f)*
	deu leh sa(n)s
gas pedal	*l'accélérateur*
	a ksay lay ra teur
gas station	*une station-service*
	sta syo(n) sehr vees
headlights	*les phares*
	far

high beams	*les feux de route*
	feu deu root
highway	*une autoroute*
	o to root
hitchhiking	*l'auto-stop (m)*
	o to stohp
on the way	*en route*
	a(n) root
regular gas	*essence ordinaire*
	eh sa(n)s ohr dee nehr
right-of-way	*priorité*
	pree o ree tay
steering wheel	*le volant*
	voh la(n)
stop light	*le feu rouge*
	feu roozh
street.	*la rue*
	roo
toll	*un péage*
	pay azh
traffic jam	*un embouteillage*
	a(n) boo tay yazh
trip.	*une excursion*
	eh ksoor zyo(n)
turn signal.	*le clignotant*
	klee nyoh ta(n)
windshield	*un pare-brise*
	par breez
windshield wipers . . .	*les essuie-glaces*
	eh swee glas

Ⓔ Essential

Driving in France will be different than what you're used to. On country roads, where you might expect one car at a time to pass another, four or five cars may pass all at once. In cities, be aware that at intersections without stoplights, or stop or yield signs, right-of-way is given to cars coming from your right. Likewise, you have right-of-way over cars to your left at this type of intersection. Just be extra vigilant and you shouldn't have any problems.

Useful Driving Verbs

To round out this chapter on transportation, here are some essential verbs related to driving.

to cross	*traverser*	
	tra vehr say	
to drive	*conduire*	
	ko(n) dweer	
to fill up	*faire le plein*	
	fehr leu pleh(n)	
to go, move.	*circuler*	
	seer koo lay	
to park.	*stationner*	
	sta syo nay	
to pass.	*doubler*	
	doo blay	
to turn	*tourner*	
	toor nay	

Chapter 7
Time for Dinner

Eating out can be either a wonderful experience or a terrible one. This chapter includes essential phrases to help you figure out what's on the menu and order it correctly.

Eating Out

First, here are some general words and phrases related to eating out.

Meals and Courses

meal	*le repas*
	reu pa
breakfast.	*le petit-déjeuner*
	peu tee day zheu nay
lunch	*le déjeuner*
	day zheu nay
dinner	*le dîner*
	dee nay
snack	*le goûter*
	goo tay
appetizers	*les hors-d'oeuvre*
	ohr deuvr
starter	*l'entrée*
	a(n) tray
soup	*la soupe, le potage*
	soop; poh tazh
main course.	*le plat principal*
	pla preh(n) see pal
salad.	*la salade*
	sa lad
dessert	*le dessert*
	deh sehr

ⓔ Essential

The word "entrée" is a false cognate. It refers to the starter in French, while in English it tends to indicate the main course. To remember what it means in French, think "entrance"—the *entrée* is the entrance to the meal.

At the Restaurant

restaurant	*le restaurant*
	reh sto ra(n)
café	*un café*
	ka fay
kitchen	*la cuisine*
	kwee zeen
dining room	*la salle à manger*
	sa la ma(n) zhay
waiter	*le serveur*
	sehr veur
waitress	*la serveuse*
	sehr veuz
cook	*le chef*
	shehf

The word *garçon* means "boy" and should never be used to get your waiter's attention. It is no longer an acceptable term—use *Monsieur* instead.

Food Options

Before getting into the nitty gritty of ordering your meal, you need to know what your choices are, right? Take a look at the following lists of different kinds of food.

Fruit *(les fruits)*

apple.	*une pomme*
	pohm
apricot.	*un abricot*
	a bree ko
banana	*une banane*
	ba nan
blackberry	*une mûre*
	moor
blueberry	*une myrtille*
	meer teey
cherry	*une cerise*
	seu reez
grape	*un raisin*
	reh zeh(n)
grapefruit	*un pamplemousse*
	pa(n) pleu moos
lemon	*un citron*
	see tro(n)
lime	*un citron vert*
	see tro(n) vehr
orange	*une orange*
	oh ra(n)zh
peach	*une pêche*
	pehsh

pear	*une poire*
	pwar
plum	*une prune*
	proon
raspberry	*une framboise*
	fra(n) bwaz
strawberry	*une fraise*
	frehz

Vegetables *(les légumes)*

artichoke	*un artichaut*
	ar tee sho
asparagus	*les asperges (f)*
	a spehrzh
bean	*un haricot*
	a ree ko
carrot	*la carotte*
	ka roht
cauliflower	*le chou-fleur*
	shoo fleur
celery	*le céleri*
	say lree
corn	*le maïs*
	ma ees
cucumber	*le concombre*
	ko(n) ko(n)br
eggplant	*une aubergine*
	o behr zheen
lettuce	*la laitue*
	lay too

Vegetables *(les légumes)* **(continued)**

mushroom	. . . . .	*le champignon*
		sha(n) pee nyo(n)
onion	. . . .	*un oignon*
		uh nyo(n)
peas	. . . .	*les petits pois (m)*
		peu tee pwa
potato	. . . .	*la pomme de terre*
		puhm deu tehr
radish	. . . .	*le radis*
		ra dee
spinach	. . . . . .	*les épinards*
		ay pee nar
tomato	. . . .	*la tomate*
		toh mat

Ⓔ *Essential*

The partitive article is used with food and drink. To order some corn or some anchovies, you would say *du maïs or des anchois*.

Meat, Fish, Poultry *(la viande, le poisson, la volaille)*

anchovies	. . . . . .	*les anchois*
		a(n) shwa
chicken	. . . .	*le poulet*
		poo leh
fish	. . . .	*le poisson*
		pwa so(n)

ham	*le jambon*	zha(n) bo(n)
lamb	*l'agneau (m)*	a nyo
pork	*le porc*	pohr
rabbit	*le lapin*	la peh(n)
roast beef	*le rosbif*	rohs beef
sausage	*le saucisson*	so see so(n)
snails	*les escargots* (m)	eh skar go
steak	*le bifteck*	beef tehk
turkey	*la dinde*	deh(n)d
veal	*le veau*	vo

Meat Prep

rare	*bleu*	bleu
medium-rare	*saignant*	seh nya(n)
medium well-done	*à point*	a pweh(n)
well done	*bien cuit*	byeh(n) kwee

Dairy *(les produits laitiers)*

buttermilk	*le babeurre*	ba beur
butter	*le beurre*	beur
cream	*la crème*	krehm
sour cream	*la crème fraîche*	krehm frehsh
cheese	*le fromage*	froh mazh
cream cheese	*le fromage blanc*	froh mazh bla(n)
ice cream	*la glace*	glas
milk	*le lait*	leh
yogurt	*le yaourt*	ya oort

Dessert *(le dessert)*

cake	*le gâteau*	ga to
candy	*les bonbons*	bo(n) bo(n)
cheese	*le fromage*	froh mazh
chocolate	*le chocolat*	shoh koh la

chocolate mousse . . . *la mousse au chocolat*
moo so shoh koh la

cookie . . . . *le biscuit*
bee skwee

custard . . . . *la crème brûlée*
krehm broo lay

flan . . . . *la crème caramel, flan*
krehm ka ra mehl, fla(n)

fruit . . . . *les fruits* (m)
frwee

ice cream . . . . *la glace*
glas

pie . . . . *la tarte*
tart

vanilla . . . . *la vanille*
va neey

Et cetera

almond . . . . *l'amande*
a ma(n)d

bread . . . . *le pain*
peh(n)

croissant . . . . *le croissant*
krwa sa(n)

egg . . . . *l'œuf* (m)
euf

eggs . . . . *les œufs*
lay zeu

fries . . . . *les frites*
freet

Et cetera (continued)

jam	*la confiture*	
	ko(n) fee toor	
mayonnaise	*la mayonnaise*	
	ma yoh nehz	
mustard	*la moutarde*	
	moo tard	
pasta	*les pâtes*	
	paht	
peanut	*l'arachide, la cacahuète*	
	a ra sheed, ka ka weht	
pepper	*le poivre*	
	pwavr	
rice	*le riz*	
	ree	
salt	*le sel*	
	sehl	
sugar	*le sucre*	
	sukr	
toast	*le pain grillé*	
	peh(n) gree yay	
wheat	*le blé*	
	blay	

Ⓔ *Fact*

Alcoholic drinks, particularly wine, are an important part of the French menu. If you don't know much about wine, don't hesitate to ask the waiter to recommend wine to go with your meal choice. They'll be happy to help!

Beverages

To go along with your food, here are some drink choices.

beverage	*la boisson*
	bwa so(n)
beer	*la bière*
	byehr
after-dinner drink	*le digestif*
	dee zheh steef
cocktail	*un apéritif*
	a pay ree teef
coffee	*le café*
	ka fay
espresso	*un express*
	ek sprehs
hot chocolate	*le chocolat chaud*
	shoh koh la sho
juice	*le jus*
	joo
lemonade	*le citron pressé*
	see tro(n) preh say
milk	*le lait*
	leh
tea	*le thé*
	tay
water	*l'eau*
	o
wine	*le vin*
	veh(n)

Dishes and Silverware

If you need to ask for another fork or napkin, here's the vocabulary you'll need.

bowl	*un bol*	bohl
cup (tea/coffee type). .	*une tasse*	tas
fork	*une fourchette*	foor sheht
glass	*un verre*	vehr
knife	*un couteau*	koo to
napkin	*une serviette*	sehr vyeht
plate	*une assiette*	a syeht
saucer	*une soucoupe*	soo koop
spoon	*une cuiller*	kwee yehr
wine glass	*un verre à vin*	veh ra veh(n)
bottle	*une bouteille*	boo tay
can, box, tin	*une boîte*	bwat
jar, cup.	*un pot*	po

Order Your Meal

Now that you know the food vocabulary, you're ready to talk about and order your meal.

to be hungry	*avoir faim*	a vwar feh(n)
to be thirsty	*avoir soif*	a vwar swaf
to order	*commander*	kuh ma(n) day
to drink	*boire*	bwar
to eat	*manger*	ma(n) zhay
check/bill	*l'addition* (f)	a dee syo(n)
menu	*la carte*	kart
side order (not part of *le menu*)	*à la carte*	a la kart
fixed-price meal	*le menu*	meu noo
tip	*le pourboire*	poor bwar
tip included	*service compris*	sehr vees ko(n) pree
tip not included	*service non compris*	sehr vees no(n) ko(n) pree

ⓔ *Essential*

Le menu is a false cognate. In France, *le menu* refers to a fixed-price menu, with limited choices for one or more courses. The full menu is known as *la carte*. The expression *à la carte* literally means "on the menu," referring to the full menu rather than the fixed-price *menu*.

What would you like? I would like . . .
Que voudriez-vous ? Je voudrais . . .
keu voo dryay voo; zheu voo dreh

What are you having?
Que prenez-vous ?
keu preu nay voo

I'm going to have . . .
Je vais prendre . . .
zheu vay pra(n)dr

How much does . . . cost?
Combien coûte . . . ?
ko(n) byeh(n) koot

Enjoy your meal!
Bon appétit !
bo na pay tee

No smoking!
Défense de fumer !
day fa(n)s deu foo may

No pets allowed.
Les animaux sont interdits.
lay za nee mo so(n) teh(n) tehr dee

Dietary Restrictions

Traveling doesn't have to mean being forced to eat things you normally shouldn't. Use these French phrases to explain your dietary restrictions. Begin with "I am" (*je suis*, pronounced "zheu swee"):

allergic to . . . . *allergique à*
a lehr zheek a
diabetic . . . . *diabétique*
dya bay teek
on a diet. . . . . *au régime*
o ray zheem
vegetarian. . . . . . . *végétarien/végétarienne*
vay zhay ta ryeh(n)/
vay zhay ta ryeh(n)(n)

I can't eat . . .
Je ne peux pas manger . . .
zheu neu peu pa ma(n) zhay

Chapter 8
Shopping and Services

Y ou may be on vacation, but life goes on as usual—your clothes are getting dirty, your hair is growing, and you might not want to eat in a restaurant three times a day. This chapter includes phrases related to stores and services.

Stores and Businesses

Take a look at this list of stores and businesses you might want to visit.

bakery	*une boulangerie*
	boo la(n) zhree
bank	*une banque*
	bahnk
butcher shop	*une boucherie*
	boo shree
candy store	*une confiserie*
	ko(n) fee zree
clothing store	*un magasin de confection*
	ma ga zeh(n) deu ko(n) feh ksyo(n)
dairy	*une laiterie*
	leh tree
department store . . .	*un grand magasin*
	gra(n) ma ga zeh(n)
drugstore	*une droguerie*
	druh gree
dry cleaner	*une teinturerie*
	ta(n) toor er ree
fish market	*une poissonnerie*
	pwa so nree
grocery store	*une épicerie*
	ay pee sree
laundromat	*une blanchisserie*
	bla(n) shee sree

🄔 Fact

Le tabac literally means "tobacco shop," but in France these little markets are also a convenient place to buy stamps, phone cards, and other small items.

newsstand	*un kiosque*	ki ohsk
outdoor market	*un marché*	mar shay
pastry shop	*une pâtisserie*	pah tee sree
pharmacy	*une pharmacie*	far ma see
pork butcher	*une charcuterie*	shar koo tree
store	*un magasin*	ma ga zeh(n)
supermarket	*un supermarché*	soo pehr mar shay
tobacco shop	*un tabac*	ta bah

Laundromat and Dry Cleaner

If you're traveling for a week or more, you'll probably need to get your clothes cleaned at some point. This vocabulary can help.

to wash	*laver*	la vay
to dry	*sécher*	say shay
to dry clean	*nettoyer à sec*	nay twa yay
bleach	*la javel*	zha vehl
change	*de la monnaie*	deu la moh neh
dryer	*le séchoir automatique*	say shwar o to ma teek
fabric softener	*l'assouplissant*	a soo plee sa(n)
laundry	*le linge*	leh(n)zh
soap	*le savon*	sa vo(n)
starch	*l'amidon*	a mee do(n)
token	*un jeton*	zheu to(n)
washing machine	*le lave-linge*	lav leh(n)zh

Hair Salon or Barbershop

Planning to get your hair done? Be sure you know how to tell the stylist what you want.

to brush	*brosser*	broh say
to blow dry	*faire le brushing*	fehr leu bruh shing
to color	*teindre*	teh(n)dr
to curl	*boucler*	boo klay
to cut	*couper*	koo pay
to perm	*faire une permanente*	fehr oon pehr ma na(n)t
to shave	*raser*	ra zay
to wash	*laver*	la vay
long	*long*	lo(n)
short	*court*	coor
too cold	*trop froide*	tro frwad
too hot	*trop chaude*	tro shod
hair stylist	*le coiffeur, la coiffeuse*	kwa feur; kwa feuz

Clothing and Jewelry

Whether shopping or doing laundry, this clothing vocabulary will come in handy.

bathing suit	*un maillot (de bain)*
	ma yo deu beh(n)
boots	*des bottes*
	boht
coat	*un manteau*
	ma(n) to
jacket	*un blouson*
	bloo zo(n)
jeans	*un jean*
	jeen
pajamas	*un pyjama*
	pee zha ma
pants	*un pantalon*
	pa(n) ta lo(n)
raincoat	*un imperméable*
	eh(n) pehr may abl
sandals	*des sandales*
	sa(n) dal
shoes	*des chaussures*
	sho soor
shorts	*un short*
	short
sneakers	*des tennis*
	tay nees
socks	*des chaussettes*
	sho seht

ski jacket	*un anorak*
	a noh rak
sweater	*un pull*
	pool
T-shirt	*un tee-shirt*
	tee sheurt

Essential

Note that *un short, un jean,* and *un pantalon* are singular,
whereas their English equivalents are plural.

Women's Clothing *(Vêtements de femme)*

bikini	*un bikini*
	bee kee nee
blouse	*un chemisier*
	sheu mee zee yay
bra	*un soutien-gorge*
	soo tyeh(n) gohrzh
dress	*une robe*
	rohb
half slip	*un jupon*
	zhoo po(n)
high-heeled shoes . .	*des chaussures à hauts talons*
	sho soor a o ta lo(n)
miniskirt	*une minijupe*
	mee nee zhoop
nightgown.	*une chemise de nuit*
	sheu meez deu nwee

Women's Clothing *(Vêtements de femme)* (continued)

panties	*un slip*	sleep
pantyhose, tights	*un collant*	koh la(n)
skirt	*une jupe*	zhoop
slip	*une combinaison*	ko(n) bee nay zo(n)
suit	*un tailleur*	ta yeur
stockings	*des bas*	ba

Men's Clothing *(Vêtements d'hommes)*

bow tie	*un nœud papillon*	neu pa pee yo(n)
boxer shorts	*un caleçon*	kal so(n)
cummerbund	*une ceinture*	seh(n) toor
shirt	*une chemise*	sheu meez
sport jacket	*une veste de sport*	vehst deu spohr
suit	*un costume*	koh stoom
tie	*une cravate*	kra vat

tuxedo.	*un smoking*
	smoh keeng
undershirt	*un maillot de corps*
	ma yo deu kuhr
underwear	*des sous-vêtements*
	soo veht ma(n)

Jewelry *(Bijoux)*

barrette	*une barrette*
	ba reht
bracelet	*un bracelet*
	bra sleh
brooch	*une broche*
	brohsh
charm bracelet	*un bracelet à breloques*
	bra sleh a breu luhk
cufflink	*un bouton de manchette*
	boo to(n) deu ma(n) sheht
earring	*une boucle d'oreille*
	bookl doh ray
engagement ring . . .	*une bague de fiançailles*
	bag deu fya(n) sahy
necklace	*un collier*
	koh lyay
pendant	*un pendentif*
	pa(n) da(n) teef
pin	*une épingle*
	ay peh(n)gl
ring	*une bague*
	bag

Jewelry *(Bijoux)* (continued)

tie pin	*une épingle de cravate*
	feeks kra vat
watch	*une montre*
	mo(n)tr
wedding ring	*une alliance*
	a lya(n)s

Accessories *(Accessoires)*

backpack	*un sac à dos*
	sa ka do
belt	*une ceinture*
	seh(n) toor
briefcase	*un porte-documents*
	pohrt do koo ma(n)
eyeglasses	*des lunettes*
	loo neht
gloves	*des gants*
	ga(n)
handkerchief	*un mouchoir*
	moo shwar
hat	*un chapeau*
	sha po
mittens	*des moufles*
	moofl
muffler	*un cache-nez*
	kash nay
purse	*un sac à main*
	sa ka meh(n)

ribbon	*un ruban*	
	roo ba(n)	
scarf	*un foulard*	
	foo lar	
shawl	*un châle*	
	shahl	
sunglasses.	*des lunettes de soleil*	
	loo neht deu soh lay	
umbrella.	*un parapluie*	
	pa ra plwee	
wallet	*un portefeuille*	
	puhrt feuy	

Colors and Sizes

Colors, like all French adjectives, have to agree with the nouns they modify.

 Fact

> Since this book is mainly for speaking purposes, the color table provides the feminine form of the adjective only when its pronunciation is different than the masculine.

Colors *(Couleurs)*

purple	*violet(te)*	
	vyuh leh/leht	
blue	*bleu*	
	bleu	

Colors *(Couleurs)* (continued)

green	. . . .	*vert(e)*
		vehr/vehrt
yellow	. . . .	*jaune*
		zhon
orange	. . . .	*orange*
		uh ra(n)zh
red	. . . .	*rouge*
		roozh
black	. . . .	*noir*
		nwar
white	. . . .	*blanc(he)*
		bla(n)/bla(n)sh
grey	. . . .	*gris(e)*
		gree/greez
brown	. . . .	*marron*
		ma ro(n)
pink	. . . .	*rose*
		roz
light blue	. . . . . .	*bleu clair*
		bleu klehr
dark blue	. . . . . .	*bleu foncé*
		bleu fo(n) say

Sizes *(Tailles)*

clothing size	. . . . .	*la taille*
		tahy
shoe size	. . . .	*la pointure*
		pweh(n) toor

What size do you wear? I wear a size . . .
Quelle taille faites-vous ? Je fais du . . .
kel tahy feht voo; zheu feh doo

French clothing and shoe sizes are numbered according to a different system than American and British, so you'll need to find a chart of equivalents. If you don't know the numerical size or if you've tried something on and need a different size, you can use the following vocabulary:

large . . . . *grand*
              gra(n)
larger . . . . *plus grand*
              ploo gra(n)
medium . . . . *moyen*
              mwa yeh(n)
small . . . . *petit*
              peu tee
smaller . . . . *plus petit*
              ploo peu tee

Chapter 9
Out on the Town

So you went shopping, bought some new clothes, got a haircut—now it's time to have some fun. There's a lot you can do: play games, watch sports, take in a movie or play—whatever interests you. In order to talk about all this, you'll need to start by learning some verbs for active and passive participation.

Active Verbs

Active verbs are the ones you'll use to describe something that you are actually participating in, as opposed to being a spectator. The active verbs that will come in most useful when talking about entertainment are *faire* (to do, make) and *jouer* (to play).

The Verb *Faire*

	Past	Present
j'/je	*ai fait* [ay fay]	*fais* [fay]
tu	*as fait* [a fay]	*fais* [fay]
il	*a fait* [a fay]	*fait* [fay]
nous	*avons fait* [a vo(n) fay]	*faisons* [feu zo(n)]
vous	*avez fait* [a vay fay]	*faites* [feht]
ils	*ont fait* [o(n) fay]	*font* [fo(n)]

What are you doing?
Que fais-tu ?
keu fay too

I'm making my bed.
Je fais mon lit.
zheu fay mo(n) lee

In French, idiomatic expressions made up of a verb + noun are often used where a simple verb exists in English. One French verb used in this way is *faire*, which is commonly followed by a noun to indicate someone performing the action of that noun:

He likes to sail.
Il aime faire de la voile.
ee lehm fehr deu la vwal

Don't pout.
Ne fais pas la moue.
neu fay pa la moo

The Verb *Jouer*

	Past	Present
j'/je	*ai joué* [ay zhoo ay]	*joue* [zhoo]
tu	*as joué* [a zhoo ay]	*joues* [zhoo]
il	*a joué* [a zhoo ay]	*joue* [zhoo]
nous	*avons joué* [a vo(n) zhoo ay]	*jouons* [zhoo o(n)]
vous	*avez joué* [a vay zhoo ay]	*jouez* [zhoo ay]
ils	*ont joué* [o(n) zhoo ay]	*jouent* [zhoo]

The verb *jouer* is used more or less like its English equivalent—with sports, games, and musical instruments. The only tricky part is that the preposition which follows *jouer* depends on what is being played. With sports and games, use the preposition *à*. With musical instruments, use *de*.

Do you play tennis?
Joues-tu au tennis ?
zhoo too o tay nees

I play the piano.
Je joue du piano.
zheu zhoo doo pya no

Ⓔ *Essential*

Note that the definite article is used in front of the thing being played, and thus *jouer* is often followed by a contraction (see Chapter 1).

Passive Verbs

When you like to sit back and watch others do something, the passive verbs *regarder* (to watch) and *voir* (to see) will be useful.

The Verb *Regarder*

Regarder is used to talk about watching television, movies, sports, etc.

He watched a movie.
Il a regardé un film.
ee la reu gar day uh(n) feelm.

I like watching tennis.
J'aime regarder le tennis.
zhehm reu gar day leu tay nees

Past	Present

j'/je

   ai regardé [ay re gar day]   *regarde* [reu gard]

tu

   as regardé [a re gar d ay]   *regardes* [reu gard]

il

   a regardé [a re gar d ay]   *regarde* [reu gard]

nous

   avons regardé [a vo(n) re gar d ay]

                              regardons [reu gar do(n)]

vous

   avez regardé [a vay re gar d ay]   *regardez* [reu gar day]

ils

   ont regardé [o(n) re gar d ay]   *regardent* [reu gard]

The Verb *Voir*

Voir is used with movies, sports, and theater.

I saw the tennis game.
J'ai vu le match de tennis.
zhay voo leu match deu tay nees

He's going to see a play.
Il va voir une pièce.
eel va vwar oon pyehs

	Past	**Present**
j'/je	*ai vu* [ay voo]	*vois* [vwa]
tu	*as vu* [a voo]	*vois* [vwa]
il	*a vu* [a voo]	*voit* [vwa]
nous	*avons vu* [a vo(n) voo]	*voyons* [vwa yo(n)]
vous	*avez vu* [a vay voo]	*voyez* [vwa yay]
ils	*ont vu* [o(n) voo]	*voient* [vwa]

Sports and Games

To talk about playing a sport or game in French, use *jouer à* + the name of the sport or game.

baseball	*le base-ball*	behz bol
basketball	*le basket*	bas keht
cards.	*les cartes*	cart
chess	*les échecs*	ay shehk
football	*le football américain*	foot bol a may ree keh(n)
golf.	*le golf*	gulf
hockey	*le hockey*	uh keh
soccer	*le football*	foot bol
tennis	*le tennis*	tay nees

volleyball . . . . *le volley(ball)*
                  voh lay (bol)

 Alert!

> Note that *le football* (or *le foot*) refers to soccer, while
> the American sport of football is translated as *le football
> américain*.

Faire de is used in front of the names of many non-
game sports, where in English you would just use a verb.
For example, "I skate" or "I am skating" would be translated as *Je fais du patinage.* "I box" or "I am boxing" would
be translated as *Je fais de la boxe.* The following chart lists
other activity nouns which are used with *faire de.* The few
specific French verbs that exist are listed in parentheses.

biking . . . . *le cyclisme, le vélo*
                  see kleezm; vay lo
boxing. . . . . *la boxe*
                  buks
hiking . . . . *la randonnée*
                  ra(n) duh nay
jogging . . . . *le jogging*
                  juh geeng
rollerskating . . . . . *le patin à roulettes*
                  pa teh(n) a roo leht
sailing . . . . *la voile*
                  vwal

skating. . . . . *le patinage*
pa tee nazh

skiing . . . . *le ski (skier)*
skee

cross-country skiing . . . *le ski de randonnée/fond*
skee deu ra(n) duh nay/fo(n)

downhill skiing . . . . . . *le ski de descente/piste*
skee deu deh sa(n)t/peest

water skiing . . . . *le ski nautique*
skee no teek

swimming. . . . . *la natation (nager)*
na ta syo(n)

wrestling . . . . *la lutte (lutter)*
loot

Other Hobbies

If you have hobbies other than sports and games, the following vocabulary will be useful to you. Note that many of these use the verb *faire* as well.

cooking . . . . *la cuisine*
kwee zeen

to cook . . . . *cuisiner*
kwee zee nay

dancing . . . . *la danse*
da(n)s

to dance. . . . . *danser*
da(n) say

fishing . . . . *la pêche*
pehsh

to fish	*pêcher*
	peh shay
to go fishing	*aller à la pêche*
	a lay a la pehsh
gardening	*le jardinage*
	zhar dee nazh
to garden	*jardiner*
	zhar dee nay
hunting	*la chasse*
	shas
to hunt	*chasser*
	sha say
music	*la musique*
	moo zeek
to listen to music	*écouter de la musique*
	ay koo tay deu la moo zeek
to play music	*jouer de la musique*
	zhoo ay deu la moo zeek
flute	*la flûte*
	floot
guitar	*la guitare*
	gee tar
piano	*le piano*
	pya no
saxophone	*le saxophone*
	sa kso fuhn
trumpet	*la trompette*
	tro(n) peht
violin	*le violon*
	vyo lo(n)

reading . . . . *la lecture*
lehk toor

to read . . . . *lire*
leer

Movies and Television

If you enjoy passive activities, you'll want to take a leisurely look at this vocabulary related to movies and television.

movie . . . . *le film*
feelm

to watch a movie . . *regarder un film*
reu gar day uh(n) feelm

movie theater . . . . . *le cinéma*
see nay ma

time/showing . . . . . *la séance*
say a(n)s

seat . . . . *la place*
plas

television . . . . *la télévision*
tay lay vee zyo(n)

TV . . . . *la télé*
tay lay

to watch TV . . . . . *regarder la télé*
reu gar day la tay lay

dubbed . . . . *doublé*
doo blay

subtitled . . . . *sous-titré*
soo tee tray

ⓔ *Question?*

Is there a way to tell the difference between subtitled and dubbed films?

The abbreviation *VO* for *version originale* indicates that the movie is in the original language with French subtitles; *VF* stands for *version française,* meaning that the movie is dubbed in French.

Live Performances

Or maybe you like to watch live performances? In that case, you'll be glad to know the following vocabulary.

theater.	*le théâtre*
	tay atr
opera	*l'opéra*
	uh pay ra
symphony.	*la symphonie*
	seh(n) fuh nee
dance	*la danse*
	da(n)s
show/performance. .	*le spectacle*
	spehk takl
balcony	*le balcon*
	bal ko(n)
orchestra	*l'orchestre*
	ohr kehstr

Chapter 10
French for Business

Whether you work in France or are dealing with people who do, knowing some business French phrases will definitely come in handy. Learn how to talk about professions, work situations, office equipment, banking, changing money, and school.

Jobs and Professions

A chapter on French for business obviously needs to start with professions, but this vocabulary may be less commonly used than you expect. In France, one's profession is sometimes considered personal information, akin to how Americans feel about how much money one earns. To be on the safe side, don't ask new French acquaintances what they do for a living unless you've been asked first.

actor	*un acteur*
	ak teur
actress	*une actrice*
	ak trees
artist	*un(e) artiste*
	ar teest
baker	*un boulanger, une boulangère*
	boo la(n) zhay; boo la(n) zhehr
butcher	*un boucher*
	boo shay
carpenter	*un charpentier*
	shar pa(n) tyay
cashier	*un caissier, une caissière*
	keh syay; keh syehr
civil servant	*un(e) fonctionnaire*
	fo(n) ksyo(n) nehr
cook	*un chef*
	shef
dentist	*un(e) dentiste*
	da(n) teest

doctor . . . . *un médecin*
　　　　　　　　　　may deu seh(n)

electrician. . . . . . . *un électricien*
　　　　　　　　　　ay lehk tree syeh(n)

employee . . . . *un(e) employé(e)*
　　　　　　　　　　a(n) plwa yay

engineer. . . . . *un ingénieur*
　　　　　　　　　　eh(n) zhay nyeur

fireman . . . . *un pompier*
　　　　　　　　　　po(n) pyay

lawyer, barrister . . . *un(e) avocat(e)*
　　　　　　　　　　a voh ka(t)

maid . . . . *une femme de chambre*
　　　　　　　　　　fam deu sha(n) br

manager. . . . . *un gérant, un(e) responsable*
　　　　　　　　　　zhay ra(n); reu spo(n) sabl

mechanic . . . . . . *un mécanicien*
　　　　　　　　　　may ka nee syeh(n)

nurse. . . . . *un infirmier (une infirmière)*
　　　　　　　　　　eh(n) feer myay; eh(n) feer myehr

pharmacist . . . . . . *un(e) pharmacien(ne)*
　　　　　　　　　　far ma syeh(n)/syehn

plumber . . . . *un plombier*
　　　　　　　　　　plo(n) byay

police officer. . . . . *un policier*
　　　　　　　　　　poh lee syay

receptionist . . . . . . *un(e) réceptionniste*
　　　　　　　　　　ray sehp syuh neest

secretary . . . . *un(e) secrétaire*
　　　　　　　　　　seu kray tehr

student	*un(e) étudiant(e)*
	ay tu dya(n)/dya(n)t
teacher	*un professeur*
	proh feu seur
waiter (waitress)	*un serveur, une serveuse*
	sehr veur; seur veuz
writer	*un(e) écrivain(e)*
	ay kree veh(n)/veh (n)n

Fact

As explained in Chapter 2, all French nouns have a gender. When talking about professions, gender can be a bit tricky, because there are a number of professions which are always masculine, even when the person in question is female. This chart of professions lists the feminine form of the profession, if any, in parentheses. If there are no parentheses, the noun is always masculine.

French at Work

Need to communicate with a French-speaking colleague? Here is an introduction to some basic French vocabulary related to employment and earnings.

boss, manager	*le chef*
	shehf
business card	*une carte de visite*
	kart deu vee zeet

CEO	*le directeur général*
	dee rehk teur zhay nay ral
company.	*une société*
	soh see ay tay
contract	*un contrat*
	ko(n) tra
interview	*un entretien*
	a(n) treu tyeh(n)
job	*un emploi, un boulot (inf.)*
	a(n) plwa; boo lo
meeting	*une réunion*
	ray oo nyo(n)
minimum wage . . .	*le SMIC*
	smeek
raise	*une augmentation de salaire*
	og ma(n) ta syo(n) deu sa lehr
résumé	*un C.V.*
	say vay
salary	*le salaire*
	sal ehr
unemployment	*le chômage*
	sho mazh
unemployed	*au chômage*
	o sho mazh
wages	*la paie*
	pehy
to apply for a job . . .	*faire une demande d'emploi*
	fehr oon deu ma(n)d da(n) plwa
to hire	*embaucher*
	a(n) bo shay

to fire . . . . *renvoyer*
                     ra(n) vwa yay
to lay off . . . . *licencier*
                     lee sa(n) syay
to work . . . . *travailler*
                     tra va yay

Alert!

Note that "salary" and *le salaire* are false cognates. "Salary" indicates fixed payment for a given period of time, whereas *le salaire* refers to payment in general, either salary or hourly wages.

On the Phone

Talking on the phone in French can be very tricky. In addition to all of the usual problems when speaking a foreign language, something about being on the phone makes comprehension more difficult. Knowing the correct French formulas for talking on the phone can help. To start, you'll need to know that when the French pick up the phone, they say *Allô ?* (pronounced "a lo").

    May I speak to . . . ?
    Pourrais-je parler à . . . ?
    poo reh zheu par lay a

I'd like to speak to . . . .
Je voudrais parler à . . . .
zhe voo dreh par lay a

Who is calling? . . . is calling.
C'est de la part de qui ? C'est de la part de . . . .
say deu la par de kee; say deu la par deu

Who is calling? This is . . . .
Qui est à l'appareil ? C'est . . . à l'appareil.
kee ay ta la pa rehy; say . . . a la pa rehy

Please hold.
Ne quittez pas.
neu kee tay pa

I'm transferring your call.
Je vous le passe.
zheu voo leu pas

The line is busy.
La ligne est occupée.
la lee nyay toh koo pay

phone number	*un numéro de téléphone*	
	noo may ro deu tay lay fuhn	
phone book	*un annuaire*	
	a nwehr	
dial tone	*la tonalité*	
	toh na lee tay	
phone booth	*une cabine téléphonique*	
	ka been tay lay foh neek	

collect call	*un appel en P.C.V.*
	a peh la(n) pay say vay
answering machine . .	*un répondeur téléphonique*
	ray po(n) deur tay lay foh neek
to call	*appeler, téléphoner à*
	a peu lay; tay lay fuh nay a
to call back	*rappeler*
	ra peu lay
to be cut off	*être coupé*
	etr koo pay
to dial a number	*composer un numéro*
	ko(n) po zay uh(n) noo may ro
to hang up	*raccrocher*
	ra kroh shay
to leave a message . . .	*laisser un message*
	leh say uh(n) may sazh
to pick up (the phone)	*décrocher*
	day kroh shay
to ring	*sonner*
	suh nay

Ⓔ *Essential*

There is a simple French gesture that can be used along with just about any kind of statement related to a phone call, such as "I'll call you" and "There's a call for you." Make a fist and extend your thumb and pinky so that your hand looks like a Y and hold it up to your ear. *Voilà le téléphone!*

Office Supplies and Equipment

How can you get any work done if you don't have the right supplies? Use this French vocabulary to equip your office.

desk, office . . . . *un bureau*
boo ro

inbox . . . . *le courrier arrivé*
koo ryay a ree vay

outbox. . . . . *le courrier départ*
koo ryay day par

pen. . . . . *un stylo*
stee lo

pencil . . . . *un crayon*
kreh yo(n)

highlighter . . . . . . *un surligneur*
sur lee nyeur

stapler . . . . *une agrafeuse*
a gra feuz

staple . . . . *une agrafe*
a graf

paper clip . . . . . . *un trombone*
tro(n) buhn

paper. . . . . *le papier*
pa pyay

piece of paper . . . . *une feuille de papier*
feuy deu pa pyay

filing cabinet . . . . . *un classeur*
kla seur

file folder . . . . *une chemise*
sheu meez

computer. . . . . *un ordinateur*
ohr dee na teur

printer . . . . *une imprimante*
eh(n) pree ma(n)t

copy machine . . . . *une photocopieuse*
foh toh koh pyeuz

fax machine. . . . . . *un télécopieur*
tay lay koh pyeur

typewriter. . . . . . . *une machine à écrire*
ma shee na ay kreer

adding machine . . . *une machine à calculer*
ma shee na kal koo lay

calculator . . . . *une calculatrice*
kal koo la trees

telephone . . . . *un téléphone*
tay lay fohn

cell phone. . . . . . . *un mobile*
moh beel

email. . . . . *le courriel*
koo ryehl

Fact

There is a great deal of English vocabulary in French (sometimes referred to as "franglais"), especially in business French. The vocabulary in this book is the "correct" French, but you should be aware that English may be used instead. Two notable examples are "fax" and "e-mail," which are often used in place of the French terms *télécopieur* and *courriel*.

Banking and Changing Money

Money makes the world go round, and when you're traveling, money is essential for letting you go round too. The following vocabulary can help you to indicate your preferred method of payment, change money, and deal with bank accounts.

money	*de l'argent*
	ar zha(n)
bill, note, paper money . .	*un billet*
	bee yay
cash	*des espèces / du liquide*
	eh spehs / lee keed
change	*la monnaie*
	moh neh
coin	*une pièce (de monnaie)*
	pyehs
check, cheque	*un chèque*
	shehk
checkbook	*un carnet de chèques*
	kar neh deu shehk
certified check	*un chèque certifié*
	shehk sehr tee fyay
traveler's check	*un chèque de voyage*
	shek deu vwa yazh
bank card, ATM card	*une carte bancaire*
	kart ba(n) kerh
credit card	*une carte de crédit*
	kart deu cray dee

bank	*une banque* ba(n)k
currency exchange. . . .	*un bureau de change* boo ro deu shanzh
ATM machine, cash dispenser	*un guichet* *automatique bancaire* gee shay o toh ma teek de ba(n)kehr
checking account	*un compte-chèques* ko(n)t shehk
savings account	*un compte d'épargne* ko(n)t day par nyeu
balance	*le solde* sohld
bank statement	*un relevé de compte* reu leu vay deu ko(n)t
exchange rate.	*le taux de change* to deu sha(n)zh
fees.	*les frais* freh
interest rate	*le taux d'intérêt* to deh(n) tay reh
loan	*un emprunt* a(n) pruh(n)
receipt	*un reçu* reu soo
sum, amount, total	*le montant* mo(n) ta(n)
yield	*le rendement* ra(n) deu ma(n)

ⓔ *Essential*

> In France, you don't necessarily have to go to a bank to manage your money. *La poste* (the post office) also offers checking and savings accounts.

to buy	*acheter*
	ash tay
to cash a check . . .	*encaisser un chèque*
	a(n) kehsay un shehk
to change money . .	*changer de l'argent (en euros)*
(into euros)	sha(n) zhay deu lar zha(n) a(n) neuro
to count	*compter*
	ko(n) tay
to deposit	*déposer (sur un compte)*
(into an account)	day poh zay [sur uh(n) ko(n)t]
to earn	*gagner*
	ga nyay
to need	*avoir besoin de*
	a vwar beu zwa(n) deu
to pay	*payer*
	pay ay
to save money	*faire des économies*
	fehr day zay koh noh mee
to sell	*vendre*
	va(n)dr
to sign	*signer*
	see nyay

to spend . . . . *dépenser*
day pa(n) say

to write a check . . . *faire un chèque*
fehr uh(n) shehk

to withdraw . . . . . . *retirer*
reu tee ray

In School

If you're not part of the business world just yet, you may
find this French vocabulary related to school more useful.

school . . . . *une école*
ay kohl

high school . . . . . . *un lycée*
lee say

college, university . . *une université*
oo nee vehr see tay

backpack . . . . *un sac à dos*
sa ka do

binder . . . . *un classeur*
kla seur

book . . . . *un livre*
leevr

chalk . . . . *une craie*
creh

chalkboard . . . . . . *un tableau*
ta blo

classroom . . . . *une salle de classe*
sal deu klas

course	*un cours*
	koor
dictionary	*un dictionnaire*
	deek syo nehr
eraser	*une gomme*
	gohm
homework	*des devoirs*
	deu vwar
junior high school	*un collège*
	koh lehzh
map	*une carte*
	kart
notebook	*un cahier*
	ka yay
paper	*le papier*
	pa pyay
piece of paper	*une feuille de papier*
	feuy deu pa pyay
pen	*un stylo*
	stee lo
pencil	*un crayon*
	kreh yo(n)
student desk	*un pupitre*
	poo peetr
test	*un examen*
	eh gza meh(n)
diploma	*un diplôme*
	dee plom

three-year/bachelor's degree . . . *une licence*
lee sa(n)s

bachelor's/master's degree . . . . *une maîtrise*
meh treez

doctorate degree . . . . *un doctorat*
dok to ra

Ⓔ *Fact*

The French equivalents given for the different types of
degrees are approximate. Because school systems vary
from country to country, there is no exact translation for
bachelor's, master's, and doctorate degrees in French.

Chapter 11
Medical French Phrases

Hopefully you won't need to go to the doctor, dentist, or police station while traveling, but if you do, it will be helpful to know these French phrases related to illness, medicine, and emergencies.

Common Ailments

These French phrases related to common ailments can help you get the right medical assistance. The following vocabulary goes with *avoir* (to have); for example, "to have arthritis" is *avoir de l'arthrite*.

arthritis	*de l'arthrite*
	ar treet
diarrhea	*la diarrhée*
	dya ray
an earache	*mal à l'oreille*
	ma la luh ray
a fever	*de la fièvre*
	fyevr
the flu	*la grippe*
	greep
frostbite	*des engelures*
	a(n) zheu loor
hay fever.	*un rhume des foins*
	rum day fwa(n)
a headache	*mal à la tête*
	ma la la teht
heartburn	*des brûlures d'estomac*
	broo loor deh stuh ma
hemorrhoids	*des hémorroïdes*
	ay muh ruh eed
motion sickness . . .	*le mal des transports*
	mal day tra(n) spuhr
a runny nose	*le nez qui coule*
	nay kee cool
sinusitis	*(de) la sinusite*
	see noo zeet
a stomachache	*mal à l'estomac*
	ma la leh stuh ma

Another group of illnesses goes with *être* (to be): for example, "to be asthmatic" is *être asthmatique*.

asthmatic	*asthmatique*
	as ma teek
(having) a cold	*enrhumé*
	a(n) roo may
diabetic	*diabétique*
	etre dya bay teek
insomniac.	*insomniaque*
	eh(n) suhm nyak

Here is the rest of the vocabulary for describing your illness:

to need an inhaler . .	*avoir besoin d'un inhalateur*
	a vwar beu zwe(n) duh(n)
	ee na la teur
to need sugar now . .	*avoir besoin de sucre*
	immédiatement
	a vwar beu zwa(n) deu sookr
	ee may dyat ma(n)
to have high	*faire de l'hypertension*
blood pressure	fehr deu lee pehr ta(n) syo(n)
to have low	*faire de l'hypotension*
blood pressure	fehr deu lee po ta(n) syo(n)
to break one's	*se casser le bras, la jambe*
arm, leg	seu ca say leu bra, la zha(n)b

E Alert!

Generally speaking, the French don't use possessive adjectives with body parts, as in "my arm" or "his leg." Instead, they use reflexive verbs: *Je me suis cassé le bras.* (I broke my arm.) *Il s'est cassé la jambe.* (He broke his leg.)

Parts of the Body

Knowing how to say the parts of the body in French will come in handy in many situations.

hair . . . . *les cheveux*
sheu veu

head . . . . *la tête*
teht

face. . . . . *le visage*
vee zazh

eye . . . . *un œil*
euy

eyes . . . . *les yeux*
zyeu

nose . . . . *le nez*
nay

cheek . . . . *la joue*
zhoo

mouth . . . . *la bouche*
boosh

lip	*la lèvre*	lehvr
tooth	*la dent*	da(n)
ear	*une oreille*	uh rehy
neck	*le cou*	koo
chest	*la poitrine*	pwa treen
stomach	*un estomac*	eh stuh ma
arm	*le bras*	bra
shoulder	*une épaule*	ay pol
elbow	*le coude*	kood
wrist	*le poignet*	pwa nyeh
hand	*la main*	meh(n)
finger	*le doigt*	dwa
fingernail	*un ongle*	o(n)gl
thumb	*le pouce*	poos
back	*le dos*	do

leg	la jambe
	zha(n)b
knee	le genou
	zheu noo
ankle	la cheville
	sheu veey
foot	le pied
	pyay
toe	un orteil
	uhr tay

Going to the Doctor

If you need to see a doctor while traveling, the following vocabulary, in conjunction with the common ailments section, above, can help you to describe your symptoms.

To Be . . . *(avoir)*

cold	froid
	frwa
dizzy	le vertige
	vehr teezh
hot	chaud
	sho
seasick	le mal de mer
	mal deu mehr
sunburnt	un coup de soleil
	coo deu suh lay

To Be . . . *(être)*

constipated	*constipé*
	ko(n) stee pay
jet lagged	*fatigué dû au décalage horaire*
	fa tee gay doo o day ka lazh
	uh rehr
pregnant.	*enceinte*
	a(n) seh(n)t
sick	*malade*
	ma lad
tired	*fatigué*
	fa tee gay

If you have an allergy, use the following phrase:

I am allergic to . . .
Je suis allergique à . . .
zheu swee a lehr zhee ka

aspirin	*l'aspirine*
	a spee reen
iodine	*l'iode*
	yuhd
penicillin.	*la pénicilline*
	pay nee see leen

Ⓔ *Essential*

If you are allergic to some kind of food, be sure to go back to Chapter 7 and memorize the French word for it.

Symptomatic Verbs

to ache all over	*avoir mal partout*	
	a vwar mal par too	
to bleed	*saigner*	
	seh nyay	
to cough	*tousser*	
	too say	
to faint	*s'évanouir*	
	say va nweer	
to fall	*tomber*	
	to(n) bay	
to sneeze	*éternuer*	
	ay tehr nway	
to throw up	*vomir*	
	vuh meer	

Going to the Dentist

The dentist's office is another place in which you definitely want to be able to communicate effectively. Here is some essential French vocabulary for talking to a dentist.

at the dentist's office	*chez le dentiste*	
	shay leu da(n) teest	
tooth	*la dent*	
	da(n)	
baby tooth	*la dent de lait*	
	da(n) deu leh	
back tooth	*la dent du fond*	
	da(n) doo fo(n)	

canine tooth	*la canine*	ka neen
front tooth	*l'incisive*	ehn seez eev(e)
lower tooth	*la dent du bas*	da(n) doo ba
molar	*la molaire*	muh lehr
upper tooth	*la dent du haut*	da(n) doo o
wisdom tooth	*la dent de sagesse*	da(n) deu sa zhehs
gums	*la gencive*	zha(n) seev
jaw	*la mâchoire*	ma shwar
mouth	*la bouche*	boosh
abscess	*un abcès*	ap seh
local anesthesia	*une anesthésie locale*	a neh stay zee luh kal
broken tooth	*une dent cassée*	da(n) ka say
cavity	*une carie*	ca ree
crown	*la couronne*	koo ruhn
filling	*un plombage*	plo(n) bazh

infected	*infecté*	
	eh(n) fehk tay	
injection.	*une piqûre*	
	pee koor	
Novocain.	*la Novocaïne*	
	nuh vuh ka een	
open your mouth. . .	*ouvrez la bouche*	
	oo vray la boosh	
permanent	*définitif/définitive*	
	day fee nee teef/day fee nee teev	
root canal	*la dévitalisation*	
	day vee ta lee za syo(n)	
teeth cleaning	*le détartrage*	
	day tar trazh	
temporary.	*provisoire*	
	pruh vee zwar	
toothache	*mal aux dents*	
	ma lo da(n)	

Ⓔ *Fact*

The French preposition *chez* does not have an exact translation in English. It is most commonly used to mean "at the home/office of," as in *chez moi* (at my house) and *chez le dentiste* (at the dentist's office).

A Few Dental Verbs

to bleed	saigner
	seh nyay
to brush (one's teeth) .	se brosser (les dents)
	seu bruh say lay da(n)
to hurt	faire mal
	fehr mal
to lose	perdre
	perdr
to pull out, remove . .	arracher
	a ra shay
to replace	remplacer
	ra(n) pla say
to rinse	rincer
	reh(n) say

Going to the Pharmacy

If you need to go to a pharmacy, be sure to take along this list to help you find exactly what you're looking for.

pharmacy	*une pharmacie*
	far ma see
pharmacist	*un pharmacien/une pharmacienne*
	far ma syeh(n)/far ma syeh(nn)
antibiotics.	*des antiobiotiques*
	a(n) tee byuh teek
antiseptic	*un antiseptique*
	a(n) tee sehp teek

aspirin . . . . *une aspirine*
a spee reen

cough drop . . . . . . *une pastille contre la toux*
pa steey ko(n)tr la too

cough syrup. . . . . . *le sirop contre la toux*
see roh ko(n)tr la too

laxative . . . . *un laxatif*
lak sa teef

medicine . . . . *un médicament*
may dee ka ma(n)

pill . . . . *une pilule*
pee lool

prescription. . . . . . *une ordonnance*
uhr duh na(n)s

remedy . . . . *un remède*
reu mehd

tablet (of medicine) . *un comprimé*
ko(n) pree may

mild . . . . *léger*
lay zhay

strong . . . . *fort*
for

Emergencies and Disasters

Hopefully you won't ever need to know French emergency vocabulary, but here's some just in case you do:

Emergency! . . . . . . *Urgence !*
oor zha(n)s

Help!. . . . . *Au secours !*
o seu koor

Fire! . . . . *Au feu !*
o feu

Police! . . . . *Police !*
puh lees

Thief!. . . . . *Au voleur !*
o vuh leur

Watch out!. . . . . . . *Attention !*
a ta(n) syo(n)

accident . . . . *un accident*
a ksee da(n)

attack . . . . *une attaque*
a tak

burglary . . . . *un cambriolage*
ka(n) bree yuh lazh

crash. . . . . *une collision*
kuh lee zyo(n)

explosion . . . . *une explosion*
ehk spluh zyo(n)

fire . . . . *un feu*
feu

flood . . . . *une inondation*
ee no(n) da syo(n)

gunshot . . . . *un coup de feu*
koo deu feu

mugging. . . . . *une aggression*
a greh syo(n)

rape . . . . *un viol*
vyul

theft . . . . *un vol*
vul

to need . . . . *avoir besoin de / d'*
a vwar beu zwa(n) deu

ambulance . . . . . . *une ambulance*
a(n) boo la(n)s

doctor . . . . *un médecin*
may deu seh(n)

fireman . . . . *un pompier*
po(n) pyay

help . . . . *l'assistance*
a see sta(n)s

police officer . . . . . *un policier*
puh lee syay

to be drowning . . . *se noyer*
seu nwa yay

to be in labor . . . . . *être en train d'accoucher*
etr a(n) tra(n) da koo shay

Chapter 12
In Your Community

Now that you've learned all the French phrases for important things such as business and going to the doctor, you're probably ready to think about your everyday tasks. This chapter deals with phrases related to shopping for food, going to the post office, buying newspapers, and other sorts of around-town situations.

At the Market

There are basically two ways that you can shop for food in France. The traditional way is to go to all of the different specialized markets (*le boucher* for meat, *le marché de légumes* for vegetables) every day, which is fun but time-consuming. The other way is to buy everything at the supermarket. Whichever you decide to do, the following phrases will be useful.

grocery store	*une épicerie*	
	ay pee seu ree	
outdoor market	*le marché*	
	mar shay	
supermarket	*un supermarché*	
	soo pehr mar shay	
this one	*celui-ci*	
	seu lwee see	
that one	*celui-là*	
	seu lwee la	
these (ones)	*ceux-ci*	
	seu see	
those (ones)	*ceux-là*	
	seu la	
expensive	*cher*	
	shehr	
cheap	*pas cher*	
	pa shehr	

Ⓔ Fact

Celui and ceux are known as demonstrative pronouns, and they need to agree with the nouns they replace. Celui is masculine singular and ceux is masculine plural, but you also need to know the feminine forms, celle and celles, both pronounced (sehl). So if you are pointing to une pomme (apple), you would say celle-ci (this one, feminine) or celle-là (that one, feminine), rather than celui-ci/là (this/that one, masculine).

Quantities, Weights, Measures

Another useful set of French phrases has to do with quantities, so that you can purchase the amount you want.

How much does it weigh? It weighs . . . kilograms.
Ça pèse combien ? Ça pèse . . . kilos.
sa pehz ko(n) byeh(n); sa pehz . . . kee lo

bit, piece	*un morceau*
	muhr so
box, can	*une boîte*
	bwat
bottle	*une bouteille*
	boo tay
jar	*un pot*
	po

gram	*un gramme*	
	grahm	
kilogram	*un kilo(gramme)*	
	kee lo (grahm)	
liter	*un litre*	
	leetr	
milliliter	*un millilitre*	
	mee lee leetr	
tin	*un bidon*	
	bee doh(n)	

Ⓔ *Alert!*

The French use the metric system of grams and liters:
1 ounce is about 28 grams (in weight) or 28 milliliters
(in volume); 1 pound is a bit more than half a kilogram;
1 kilogram is about 2.2 pounds; 1 quart is a little less than
a liter, about 950 milliliters.

enough	*assez (de)*	
	a say	
a lot, many	*beaucoup (de)*	
	bo koo	
how many, much . . .	*combien (de)*	
	ko(n) byeh(n)	
more	*encore (de)*	
	a(n) kuhr	
less, fewer	*moins (de)*	
	mwe(n)	

a little	un peu (de)
	uh(n) peu
more	plus (de)
	ploo
too much, too many	trop (de)
	tro

At the Bakery

Even if you find it convenient to do most of your shopping at the supermarket, one place where you'll be happy to go every day is the bakery. Every French bakery is different and there are hundreds of different kinds of bread in all. Here are some common terms you'll need.

baker	le boulanger/la boulangère
	boo la(n) zhay/boo la(n) zhehr
bakery	la boulangerie
	boo la(n) zheu ree
bread	le pain
	peh(n)
brown bread	le pain bis
	peh(n) bee
chocolate croissant	le pain au chocolat
	peh(n) o shoh koh la
country bread	le pain de campagne
	peh(n) deu ka(n) pa nyeu
croissant	le croissant
	krwa sa(n)
French bread	la baguette
	ba geht

French bread (thin) . . *la flûte*
floot

leavened bread . . . . *le pain au levain*
(sourdough) peh(n) no leu veh(n)

rye bread . . . . *le pain de seigle*
peh(n) deu sehgl

unleavened bread . . . *le pain azyme*
peh(n) a zeem

wholegrain bread . . . *le pain complet*
peh(n) ko(n) pleh

Bread is different in France, so some of the English terms are approximations rather than exact translations.

At the Post Office

La Poste offers more than you might expect of a post office. In addition to normal post office services, the French postal system also offers postal checking accounts.

post office. . . . . *la poste*
puhst

counter, window. . . . *le guichet*
gee sheh

mail . . . . *le courrier*
koo ryay

mailbox . . . . *une boîte aux lettres*
bwat o lehtr

other destinations . . . *autres destinations*
o treu deh stee na syo(n)

stamp . . . . *un timbre*
teh(n)br

book of stamps . . . . *un carnet de timbres*
kar neh deu teh(n)br

bulk stamps . . . . . . *des timbres en gros*
teh(n)br a(n) gro

air mail . . . . *par avion*
pa ra vyo(n)

change of address . . *le changement d'adresse*
sha(n)zh ma(n) da drehs

Express mail . . . . . *Chronopost*
kro no puhst

forwarding . . . . . . *la réexpédition*
ray ehk spay dee syo(n)

general delivery . . . *la poste restante*
puhst reh sta(n)t

insured . . . . *assuré*
a soo ray

receipt . . . . *le reçu*
reu soo

registered . . . . *recommandé*
reu ko ma(n) day

return receipt . . . . *l'avis de réception*
a vee de ray sehp syo(n)

special delivery . . . . *en express*
ehk sprehs

address . . . . *une adresse*
a drehs

envelope . . . . *une enveloppe*
a(n) veu luhp

letter	*une lettre*	lehtr
package	*un paquet, un colis*	pa keh, kuh lee
post card	*une carte postale*	kart puh stal
recipient	*le destinataire*	deh stee na tehr
sender	*l'expéditeur*	ehk spay dee teur
size	*la dimension*	dee ma(n) syo(n)
weight	*le poids*	pwa
money order	*un mandat*	ma(n) dat
postal checking account	*un compte chèque postal (CCP)*	ko(n)t shehk puh stal

Ⓔ Alert!

Remember that the French keyboard has a different layout than you might be used to. If you don't know how
to use a French keyboard, ask the assistant if they can
switch it to the one you do know. The physical keyboard
will be the same, but the letters you type will be in the
order you're used to.

Computers and Cybercafés

If you don't have your own computer, going to a cybercafé is your best bet for checking email, printing documents, and surfing the net. Here is some vocabulary to help you find your way.

computer	*un ordinateur*
	uhr dee na teur
cybercafé	*un cybercafé*
	see behr ka fay
CD-ROM drive	*un lecteur de CD-ROM*
	lehk teur de say day ruhm
email.	*le courriel*
	koo ryehl
email address.	*une adresse électronique*
	a drehs ay lehk truh neek
file	*un fichier*
	fee shyay
floppy disk	*une disquette*
	dee skeht
hard drive.	*un disque dur*
	deesk door
internet	*l'Internet*
	eh(n) tehr neht
keyboard	*un clavier*
	kla vyay
laptop	*un portable*
	puhr tabl
monitor	*un moniteur*
	muh nee teur

mouse	*une souris*
	soo ree
per hour	*(de) l'heure*
	(deu) leur
printer	*une imprimante*
	eh(n) pree ma(n)t
scanner	*un scanner*
	ska nair
software	*un logiciel*
	luh zhee syehl
website	*un site web*
	seet wehb
download	*télécharger*
	tay lay shar zhay
receive	*recevoir*
	reu seu vwar
send	*envoyer*
	a(n) vwa yay

Chapter 13
Miscellaneous French

No matter how many different ways you try to organize something, it seems that there are always a few odds and ends that don't fit neatly into categories, and French phrases are no exception. This chapter combines all the topical phrases that don't fit anywhere else: weather, physical descriptions, personality, mood, possession, and love language.

Weather Words

When all else fails, you can always fall back on talking about the weather.

How's the weather? It is . . .
Quel temps fait-il ? Il fait . . .
kehl ta(n) feh teel; il feh

hot	*chaud*	sho
cold	*froid*	frwa
cool	*frais*	freh
nice out	*beau*	bo
bad weather	*mauvais*	mo veh
humid	*humide*	oo meed
heavy	*lourd*	loor
sunny	*soleil*	suh lay
cloudy	*nuageux*	nwa zheu
stormy	*orageux*	uh ra zheu

The following words may be used with "it's"—*il* (eel):

raining	*pleut*
	pleu
pouring	*pleut à verse*
	pleu a vehrs
snowing	*neige*
	nehzh
freezing	*gèle*
	zhehl
windy	*il y a du vent*
	eel ee ah doo va(n)
foggy	*il y a du brouillard*
	eel ee ah doo brwee yar

Descriptive Data

Being able to describe a person's physical attributes can come in handy in numerous situations, from telling the police about a pick-pocket to talking to your friends about a potential new boyfriend or girlfriend.

man	*un homme*
	uhm
woman	*une femme*
	fahm
boy	*un garçon*
	gar so(n)
girl	*une fille*
	feey
tall	*grand/grande*
	gra(n)/gra(n)d

short	*petit/petite*
	peu tee/peu teet
fat	*gros/grosse*
	gro/gros
thin	*mince*
	meh(n)s
handsome	*beau*
	bo
ugly	*moche*
	muhsh
tan	*bronzé/bronzée*
	bro(n) zay
pretty	*jolie*
	zhuh lee
beautiful	*belle*
	behl
eyes	*les yeux*
	zyeu
hair	*les cheveux*
	sheu veu
freckles	*des taches de rousseur*
	tash deu roo seur
dimples	*des fossettes*
	fuh seht

Personality Points

If you're describing a pick-pocket, this vocabulary won't help much, but if you're talking about a boyfriend or girl-friend, personality vocabulary is even more important than physical descriptions (well, maybe).

athletic	*sportif*
	spuhr teef
boring	*ennuyeux*
	a(n) nwee yeu
brave	*courageux*
	koo ra zheu
cowardly	*lâche*
	lash
friendly	*aimable*
	ay mabl
funny	*drôle*
	drol
hard-working	*travailleur*
	tra va yeur
impatient	*impatient*
	eh(n) pa sya(n)
interesting	*intéressant*
	eh(n) tay ray sa(n)
kind	*gentil*
	zha(n) tee
lazy	*paresseux*
	pa ray seu
mean	*méchant*
	may sha(n)
naive	*naïf*
	na eef
nice	*sympathique, sympa*
	seh(n) pa teek
open-minded	*sans préjugés*
	sa(n) pray zhu zhay

outgoing. . . . . *ouvert*
oo vehr

patient. . . . . *patient*
pa tya(n)

patriotic . . . . *patriotique*
pa tryuh teek

playful . . . . *taquin*
ta keh(n)

serious. . . . . *sérieux*
say ryeu

shy . . . . *timide*
tee meed

smart . . . . *intelligent*
eh(n) tay lee zha(n)

snobbish . . . . *snob*
snuhb

sophisticated . . . . . *raffiné*
ra fee nay

strong . . . . *fort*
fuhr

studious . . . . *studieux*
stoo dyeu

stupid . . . . *stupide*
stoo peed

unfriendly. . . . . . . *froid*
frwa

weak. . . . . *faible*
fehbl

Mood Management

Describe your mood or someone else's with this French mood vocabulary.

angry	*fâché*
	fa shay
ashamed	*avoir honte*
	a vwar o(n) teu
bored, annoyed	*ennuyé*
	a(n) nwee yay
calm	*tranquille*
	tra(n) keel
confident	*assuré*
	a soo ray
confused	*désorienté*
	day zuh rya(n) tay
delighted	*ravi*
	ra vee
distressed, sorry	*navré*
	na vray
embarassed	*confus*
	ko(n) foo
exhausted	*épuisé*
	ay pwee zay
happy	*heureux*
	eu reu
hyper(active)	*excité*
	ehk see tay
lonely	*solitaire*
	suh lee tehr

nervous . . . . *nerveux*
nehr veu

rushed, in a hurry . . *pressé*
preh say

sad . . . . *triste*
treest

scared . . . . *effrayé*
ay fray yay

tired . . . . *fatigué*
fa tee gay

worried . . . . *inquiet*
eh(n) kyeh

Love Language

What would a book of French phrases be worth if it didn't
include love language in the language of love?

I love you (too). I adore you.
Je t'aime (aussi). Je t'adore.
zheu tehm (o see); zheu ta durh

Will you marry me?
Veux-tu m'épouser ?
veu too may poo zay

to date . . . . *sortir avec*
suhr teer a vehk

to get engaged . . . . *se fiancer à*
seu fya(n) say a

to get married.	*se marier avec*
	seu ma ryay a vehk
engagement.	*les fiançailles*
	fya(n) sahy
marriage	*la vie maritale*
	vee ma ree tal
wedding.	*les noces*
	nuhs
wedding anniversary.	*l'anniversaire de mariage*
	a nee vehr sehr deu ma ryazh
honeymoon.	*la lune de miel*
	loon deu myehl
present	*un cadeau*
	ka do
flowers.	*des fleurs*
	fleur
candy	*des bonbons*
	bo(n) bo(n)
perfume	*le parfum*
	par fuh(n)
jewelry.	*des bijoux*
	bee zhoo
engagement ring . . .	*une bague de fiançailles*
	bahg deu fya(n) sahy
wedding ring	*une alliance*
	a lya(n)s
husband	*un mari*
	ma ree
spouse.	*un époux*
	ay poo

fiance	*un fiancé*	
	fya(n) say	
lover	*un amant*	
	a ma(n)	
boyfriend	*un copain*	
	kuh peh(n)	
friend	*un ami*	
	a mee	
wife	*une femme*	
	fahm	
spouse	*une épouse*	
	ay pooz	
fiancee	*une fiancée*	
	fya(n) say	
lover	*une amante*	
	a ma(n)t	
girlfriend	*une copine*	
	ku peen	
friend	*une amie*	
	a mee	

 Fact

Un copain can refer to a male friend or a boyfriend, while *une copine* can be a female friend or a girlfriend. Use a possessive article (*mon* or *ma,* for example) to make it clear you're talking about a boyfriend or girlfriend.

Chapter 14
Common French Expressions

Throughout this book, you've been presented with lists of French vocabulary and phrases organized by topic or situation. This final chapter is different in that it provides lists of common French expressions organized by verb. Some of these expressions can be more or less literally translated into English; those which cannot be literally translated are known as idiomatic expressions and are understandably more difficult to learn and remember.

Expressions with Aller

The French verb *aller* means "to go" and is an irregular verb (see chapter 5 for conjugations).

to be going to	*aller + infinitive*
to go fishing	*aller à la pêche*
to go meet someone	*aller rencontrer quelqu'un*
to go on foot	*aller à pied*
to be becoming, to suit	*aller à quelqu'un*
to go meet someone	*aller au-devant de quelqu'un*
to get to the bottom of things	*aller au fond des choses*
to match something	*aller avec quelque chose*
to get, to fetch	*aller chercher*
to go hand in hand with	*aller de pair avec*
to ride in a car	*aller en voiture*
Go ahead!	*Allez-y !*
Come on then.	*Allons donc !*
Let's go!	*Allons-y !*
How are you?	*Ça va ?*
That goes without saying	*Ça va sans dire*
How are you?	*Comment allez-vous ?*
How are you?	*Comment vas-tu ?*
Shall we go?	*On y va ?*
to go away	*s'en aller*

ⓔ *Essential*

If you need to tell someone to go away, *s'en aller* becomes *va-t-en !* On the other hand, if you want to tell someone that you'll go away (and leave them alone), say *je m'en vais*. The conjugations are pretty tricky, but these are probably the only two you'll need.

Expressions with Donner

The verb *donner* means "to give."

to guess that someone is . . . years old
donner . . . ans à quelqu'un

to be on full-blast (e.g., radio, TV)
donner à fond, à plein

to make someone think that
donner à quelqu'un à penser que

to face north/south
donner au nord/sud

to give someone an appetite
donner de l'appétit à quelqu'un

to make someone feel hungry/cold
donner faim/froid à quelqu'un

to make someone seasick
donner le mal de mer à quelqu'un

to make someone feel dizzy
donner le vertige à quelqu'un

to tell someone the time
donner l'heure à quelqu'un

to order someone to + verb
donner l'ordre à quelqu'un de + infinitive

to take something in to be repaired
donner quelque chose à *(+ a business)*

to give someone something to do
donner quelque chose à faire à quelqu'un

to trade, swap
donner quelque chose contre quelque chose

to give up one's seat
donner sa place

to offer one's friendship to someone
donner son amitié à quelqu'un

to give one's heart to someone
donner son cœur à quelqu'un

to give someone a kiss
donner un baiser à quelqu'un

to give someone a call
donner un coup de fil à quelqu'un

to help someone out
donner un coup de main à quelqu'un (informal)

to sweep/dust quickly
donner un coup de balai/chiffon

Ⓔ *Fact*

You might think that *donner* doesn't have anything to do with English, but in fact it shares an etymological root with the word "donate."

Expressions with Faire

In addition to the uses of *faire* (to do, make) with weather, sports, and musical instruments discussed elsewhere in this book, the verb *faire* is used in many common French expressions:

to pay attention to, watch out for	*faire attention à*
to welcome	*faire bon accueil*
to hitchhike	*faire de l'autostop*
to save up	*faire des économies*
to do one's best	*faire de son mieux*
to make progress	*faire des progrès*
to make plans	*faire des projets*
to do odd jobs, putter around	*faire du bricolage*
to oppose, face up to	*faire face à*
to be daylight, nightime	*faire jour, nuit*
to meet (for the first time)	*faire la connaissance de*
to cook	*faire la cuisine*
to do the laundry	*faire la lessive, le linge*

to pout, sulk	*faire la moue*
to stand in line, to line up	*faire la queue*
to sulk	*faire la tête*
to do dishes	*faire la vaisselle*
to make the bed	*faire le lit*
to do the shopping	*faire les achats*
to do housework	*faire le ménage*
to pack	*faire les bagages, valises*
to do the windows	*faire les vitres*
to run errands / to go shopping	*faire les courses*
to go / walk around	*faire le tour de*
to be a part of	*faire partie de*
to get up and get dressed, to wash up	*faire sa toilette*
to pretend to	*faire semblant de*
to say good-bye	*faire ses adieux*
to do homework	*faire ses devoirs*
to make one's bed	*faire son lit*
to do one's best	*faire son possible*
to wink at	*faire un clin d'œil à*
to make a blunder; do something stupid	*faire une bêtise*
to make a strange / funny face	*faire une drôle de tête*
to blunder, make a mistake	*faire une gaffe*
to take a walk (a ride)	*faire une promenade (en voiture)*
to make a complaint	*faire une réclamation*
to pay a visit	*faire une visite*
to take a trip	*faire un voyage*

Faire followed by a verb means "to make something happen" or "to have something done":

Le froid fait geler l'eau.
Cold makes water freeze.

Je fais laver la voiture.
I'm having the car washed.

 Fact

Faire une promenade and faire un tour both mean "to take a walk," whereas the addition of en voiture to either expression changes it to mean "to take a ride."

Expressions with Mettre

Mettre literally means "to put" and is an irregular verb: *je mets, tu mets, il met, nous mettons, vous mettez, ils mettent.*

to take 5 hours to do (something)	*mettre 5 heures à faire*
to put money into	*mettre de l'argent dans*
to spend money on	*mettre de l'argent sur*
to turn on the radio, the news	*mettre la radio, les informations*
to bring out, enhance	*mettre en relief*
to set the alarm	*mettre le réveil*
to set the table	*mettre la table/le couvert*
to bolt the door	*mettre le verrou*
to lay something down flat	*mettre quelque chose à plat*

to stand something up	*mettre quelque chose debout*
to set something straight	*mettre quelque chose droit*
to bring someone in line	*mettre quelqu'un au pas*

Expressions with **Rendre**

Rendre means "to give something back" or "to return something." With an adjective, it means "to make something" + that adjective, such as *rendre heureux* (to make happy).

to breathe one's last	*rendre l'âme*
to worship	*rendre un culte à*
to glorify	*rendre gloire à*
to repay unfairly gotten gains	*rendre gorge*
to give thanks to	*rendre grâce à*
to pay hommage to	*rendre hommage à*
to pay tribute to	*rendre honneur à*
to pay the last tributes to	*rendre les derniers honneurs à*
to give someone a head start	*rendre des points*
to give a reason for something	*rendre raison de quelque chose à*
to be a great help, to be handy	*rendre service*
to do someone a service	*rendre service à quelqu'un*
to breathe one's last	*rendre le dernier soupir*
to visit someone	*rendre visite à quelqu'un*

Impersonal Expressions

Impersonal expressions are those which do not have a specific subject. In French, the impersonal subject is expressed with either *il* or *ce*. The expressions listed here can be followed by either *de* + infinitive or *que* + subject + conjugated verb:

It's important to study.
Il est important d'étudier.

David is probably studying.
Il est probable que David étudie.

It's amazing	*Il est étonnant*
It's certain	*Il est certain*
It's doubtful	*Il est douteux*
It's good	*Il est bon*
It's important	*Il est important*
It's impossible	*Il est impossible*
It's improbable	*Il est improbable*
It's necessary	*Il est nécessaire*
It's normal	*Il est normal*
It's not likely	*Il est peu probable*
It's obvious	*Il est évident*
It's possible	*Il est possible*
It's probable	*Il est probable*
It's rare	*Il est rare*
It's regrettable	*Il est regrettable*
It's shameful	*Il est honteux*
It's sure/certain	*Il est sûr/certain*
It's time	*Il est temps*
It's too bad	*Il est dommage*
It's true	*Il est vrai*

It's useful   *Il est utile*
It's useless   *Il est inutile*

 Fact

Except for *il est temps,* all of the impersonal expressions can be used with *c'est* in place of *il est* with no change in meaning, but with a touch of informality.

Appendix A
French to English Dictionary

à bientôt	see you soon
à côté de	next to
à demain	see you tomorrow
à deux lits	with two beds
à droite	right
à gauche	left
à la carte	side order (not part of "le menu")
à la prochaine	until next time
à point	medium-rare
à tout à l'heure	see you soon
à vos / tes souhaits	bless you (after a sneeze)
à votre / ta santé	cheers
un abcès	abscess
un abricot	apricot
un accélérateur	gas pedal
un accident	accident
acheter	to buy
un acteur	actor
une actrice	actress
l'addition	check, bill
adieu	farewell
une adresse	address
une aérogare	terminal
un aéroport	airport
une affiche	poster
africain(e)	African
l'agneau	lamb
une agrafe	staple
une agrafeuse	stapler
algérien(ne)	Algerian
allemand(e)	German
aller	to go
aller + infinitive	to be going to
aller à la pêche	to go fishing

aller à pied	to go on foot
aller à quelqu'un	to be becoming, to suit
aller au fond des choses	to get to the bottom of things
aller avec quelque chose	to match something
aller chercher	to get, to fetch
aller de pair avec	to go hand in hand with
aller en voiture	to ride in a car
aller sans dire	to go without saying
s'en aller	to go away
allergique à	allergic to
Allez-y !	Go ahead!
une alliance	wedding ring
Allô ?	Hello?
Allons donc !	Come on then.
Allons-y !	Let's go!
l'amande	almond
un(e) amante	lover
une ambulance	ambulance
aimable	friendly
un(e) ami(e)	friend
les anchois	anchovies
une anesthésie locale	local anesthesia
anglais(e)	English
les animaux sont interdits	no pets allowed
l'anniversaire de mariage	wedding anniversary
un annuaire	phone book
un anorak	ski jacket
août	August
un apéritif	cocktail
un appel en P.C.V.	collect call
appeler	to call
arabe	Arabic
l'arachide	peanut
l'argent	money

une armoire	closet
arracher	to pull out, remove
l'arrêt du bus	bus stop
l'arthrite	arthritis
les arrivées	Arrivals
un artichaut	artichoke
un(e) artiste	artist
un ascenseur	elevator
asiatique	Asian
les asperges	asparagus
l'aspirine	aspirin
une assiette	plate
l'assistance	help
assuré	confident, insured
asthmatique	asthma
Attention !	Watch out!
atterrir	to land
Au feu !	Fire!
Au revoir	Good-bye
Au secours !	Help!
Au voleur !	Thief!
une aubergine	eggplant
australien(ne)	Australian
une auto	car
l'autobus	bus
automne	autumn
une autoroute	highway
l'auto-stop	hitchhiking
autres destinations	other destinations
avec	with
Avez-vous un(e) . . .	Do you have a(n) . . .
un avion	airplane
l'avis de réception	return receipt
un(e) avocat(e)	lawyer, barrister

avoir	to have
avoir . . . ans	to be . . . years old
avoir besoin de	to need
avoir besoin de sucre immédiatement	to need sugar now
avoir besoin d'un inhalateur	to need an inhaler
avoir chaud	to be hot
avoir de la chance	to be lucky
avoir envie de	to want
avoir faim	to be hungry
avoir froid	to be cold
avoir honte	to be ashamed
avoir l'air + adjective	to look . . .
avoir l'air de + noun	to look like a . . .
avoir l'intention de	to intend to
avoir mal à la tête	to have a headache
avoir mal à l'estomac	to have a stomach ache
avoir mal aux yeux	to have an eyeache
avoir mal au coeur	to be sick to one's stomach
avoir mal partout	to ache all over
avoir peur de	to be afraid of
avoir raison	to be right
avoir soif	to be thirsty
avoir sommeil	to be sleepy
avoir tort	to be wrong
avoir une attaque	to have a stroke
avoir une crise cardiaque	to have a heart attack
avril	April
le babeurre	buttermilk
les bagages	baggage
les bagages à main	carry-on luggage
les bagages enregistrés	checked luggage
une bague	ring

une bague de fiançailles	engagement ring
une baguette	French bread
la baignoire	bathtub
le bain	bath
le bain moussant	bubble bath
le balcon	balcony
une banane	banana
une banque	bank
une barrette	barrette
des bas	stockings
le base-ball	baseball
la base (de maquillage)	foundation
le basket(-ball)	basketball
un bateau	boat
le baume démêlant	hair conditioner
beau	nice weather, handsome
belge	Belgian
belle	beautiful
le beurre	butter
une bicyclette	bicycle
bien cuit	well done (meat)
la bière	beer
le bifteck	steak
des bijoux	jewelry
un bikini	bikini
un billet	paper money, note, bill, ticket
un billet aller-retour	round trip ticket
le billet d'avion	plane ticket
un billet aller	one-way ticket
le biscuit	cookie
blanc	white
la blanchisserie	laundromat
le blé	wheat
bleu	blue, rare (meat)

bleu clair	light blue
bleu foncé	dark blue
blond(e)	blond
un blouson	jacket
boire	to drink
une boîte	can, box, tin
une boîte aux lettres	mailbox
un bol	bowl
bon appétit !	enjoy your meal
des bonbons	candy
Bonjour	Hello
Bonne nuit	Good night
Bonsoir	Good evening
des bottes	boots
la bouche	mouth
un boucher	butcher
la boucherie	butcher shop
bouclé	curly
une boucle d'oreille	earring
un boulanger	baker
(une boulangère)	
la boulangerie	bakery
une bouteille	bottle
une boutique hors taxes	duty-free shop
un bouton de manchette	cufflink
la boxe	boxing
un bracelet	bracelet
un bracelet à breloques	charm bracelet
le bras	arm
brésilien(ne)	Brazilian
une broche	brooch
bronzé	tanned
la brosse à cheveux	hairbrush
la brosse à dents	toothbrush

se brosser les cheveux	to brush one's hair
se brosser les dents	to brush one's teeth
le brouillard	fog
des brûlures d'estomac	heartburn
brun	brown (hair)
un bureau	desk, office, study
un bureau de change	currency exchange
Ça bouge ?	How's it going?
Ça roule ?	How's it going?
ça va	fine
Ça va ?	How are you?
ça va bien	I'm doing well
ça va mal	not well
ça va sans dire	that goes without saying
une cabine téléphonique	phone booth
la cacahuète	peanut
un cache-nez	muffler
un cadeau	present
le café	coffee
un café	café
un cahier	notebook
un caissier (une caissière)	cashier
une calculatrice	calculator
un caleçon	boxer shorts
un camion	truck
canadien(ne)	Canadian
le canapé	sofa, couch
la canine	canine tooth
une carie	cavity
un carnet de chèques	checkbook
un carnet de timbres	book of stamps
la carotte	carrot
la carte	menu, map
une carte bancaire	ATM/bank card

une carte de crédit	credit card
la carte d'embarquement	boarding pass
une carte postale	post card
se casser le bras, la jambe	to break one's arm, leg
une casserole	baking dish
une ceinture	belt, cummerbund
le céleri	celery
cent	one hundred
une cerise	cherry
C'est . . . à l'appareil.	. . . is calling.
C'est combien ?	How much is it?
C'est . . .	It's . . .
une chaîne stéréo	stereo
une chaise	chair
un châle	shawl
la chambre	bedroom, hotel room
le champignon	mushroom
le changement d'adresse	change of address
changer de l'argent	to change money
un chapeau	hat
la charcuterie	pork butcher, deli
un chariot	cart
un charpentier	carpenter
la chasse	hunting
chasser	to hunt
chaud	hot
des chaussettes	socks
des chaussures	shoes
un chef	boss, manager
un(e) chef	cook
une chemise	file folder; men's shirt, blouse
une chemise de nuit	nightgown
un chèque	check, cheque
un chèque certifié	certified check

un chèque de voyage	traveler's check
les cheveux	hair
la cheville	ankle
chez le dentiste	at the dentist's office
chez moi	at my house
chinois(e)	Chinese
le chocolat	chocolate
le chocolat chaud	hot chocolate
le chou-fleur	cauliflower
Chronopost	Express mail
le cinéma	movie theater
cinq	five
cinquante	fifty
circuler	to go, move
un citron	lemon
le citron pressé	lemonade
un citron vert	lime
la classe touriste	coach, economy class
un classeur	binder, filing cabinet
le clignotant	turn signal
le coiffeur	barber, hairdresser
un colis	package
un collant	pantyhose, tights
un collège	junior high school
un collier	necklace
une collision	crash
une combinaison	slip
Combien coûte . . . ?	How much does . . . cost?
commander	to order
comme ci, comme ça	so-so
comment	how
Comment ?	What?
le commissariat	police station
une commode	dresser

une compagnie aérienne	airline
une copine	girlfriend
complet	no vacancy
composer un numéro	to dial a number
un compte chèque postal (CCP)	postal checking account
un compte d'épargne	savings account
un compte-chèques	checking account
compter	to count
le concombre	cucumber
un conducteur	driver
conduire	to drive
la confiserie	candy store
la confiture	jam
confus	embarassed
un congélateur	freezer
constipé	constipated
un contrat	contract
le contrôle de sécurité	security check
un copain	boyfriend
un costume	suit (man's)
le cou	neck
le coude	elbow
le couloir	hall
un coup de feu	gunshot
un coup de soleil	sunburn
courageux	brave
la couronne	crown
le courriel	email
le courrier	(postal) mail
le courrier arrivé	inbox
le courrier départ	outbox
un cours	course
court	short (length)

un(e) cousin(e)	cousin
un couteau	knife
une craie	chalk
une cravate	tie
un crayon	pencil
la crème	cream
la crème à raser	shaving cream
la crème brûlée	custard
la crème caramel	flan
la crème fraîche	very thick cream
la crème hydratante	moisturizer
un croissant	croissant
une cuiller à mesurer	measuring spoon
une cuiller	spoon
une cuillère à soupe	tablespoon
une cuillère à thé	teaspoon
la cuisine	cooking, kitchen
cuisiner	to cook
une cuisinière	stove
une culotte	panties
le cyclisme	biking
d'accord	OK
la danse	dance, dancing
danser	to dance
de rien	you're welcome
décembre	December
déclarer	to declare
décoller	to take off
décrocher	to pick up (the phone)
défense de fumer	no smoking
définitif/ve	permanent
le déjeuner	lunch
le démaquillant	make-up remover
la dent	tooth

une dent cassée	broken tooth
le dentifrice	toothpaste
un(e) dentiste	dentist
le déodorant	deodorant
les départs	Departures
dépenser	to spend
déposer	to deposit
désolé(e)	sorry
désorienté	confused
le dessert	dessert
le destinataire	recipient
le détartrage	teeth cleaning
deux	two
la dévitalisation	root canal
des devoirs	homework
diabétique	diabetic
la diarrhée	diarrhea
un dictionnaire	dictionary
le digestif	after-dinner drink
dimanche	Sunday
la dimension	size (of a package)
la dinde	turkey
le dîner	dinner
le directeur général	CEO
le dissolvant	nail polish remover
dix	ten
dix-huit	eighteen
dix-neuf	nineteen
dix-sept	seventeen
le doigt	finger
le dos	back
la douane	customs
doublé	dubbed
doubler	to pass

la douche	shower
douze	twelve
la droguerie	drugstore
drôle	funny
l'eau	water
l'eau dentifrice	mouthwash
les échecs	chess
une école	school
écouter (de) la musique	to listen to music
un écrivain	writer
effrayé	scared
l'église	church
un égouttoir	dishrack
égyptien(ne)	Egyptian
un électricien	electrician
elle	she
embarquer	to board
embaucher	to hire
un embouteillage	traffic jam
un(e) employé(e)	employee
un emprunt	loan
en arrière de	in back of
en avance	early
en avant de	in front of
en bas	down
en classe touriste	in economy class
en haut	up
en panne	broken-down
en première classe	in first class
en retard	late
en route	on the way
enceinte	pregnant
enchanté	pleased to meet you
encore une fois	one more time

des engelures	frostbite
ennuyé	annoyed, bored
ennuyeux	boring
l'enregistrement	check-in
enregistrer (les bagages)	to check bags
enrhumé	cold (illness)
une enveloppe	envelope
une épaule	shoulder
l'épicerie	grocery store
les épinards	spinach
une épingle	pin
une épingle de cravate	tie pin
une éponge	sponge
une épouse	wife
un époux	husband
épuisé	exhausted
une escale	stopover
un escalier	stairway
les escargots	snails
espagnol(e)	Spanish
des espèces	cash
l'essence	gas, petrol
essence ordinaire	regular gas
les essuie-glaces	windshield wipers
est	east
un estomac	stomach
et	and
une étagère	bookshelf
été	summer
éternuer	to sneeze
être	to be
un(e) étudiant(e)	student
européen(ne)	European
s'évanouir	to faint

un évier	sink (kitchen)
un examen	test
excité	hyper(active)
une excursion	trip
excusez-moi	excuse me
l'expéditeur	sender
une explosion	explosion
un expresso	espresso
fâché	angry
faible	weak
faire	to do, make
le fard à joues	blusher
le fard à paupières	eyeshadow
fatigué	tired
fatigué dû au décalage horaire	jet lagged
une femme	woman, wife
une femme de chambre	maid
une fenêtre	window
un feu	fire
le feu rouge	stop light
les feux de route	high beams
les feux de stop	brake lights
une feuille de papier	sheet of paper
février	February
les fiançailles	engagement
un(e) fiancé(e)	fiance(e)
se fiancer	to get engaged
la fièvre	fever
le fil dentaire	dental floss
une fille	girl, daughter
le film	movie
un fils	son
flamand	Flemish

une fleur	flower
la flûte	flute; thin French bread
un(e) fonctionnaire	civil servant
le foot(ball)	soccer
le football américain	football (US)
fort	strong
des fossettes	dimples
un foulard	scarf
un four	oven
un four à micro-ondes	microwave
une fourchette	fork
frais	cool
les frais	fees
une fraise	strawberry
une framboise	raspberry
français(e)	French
les freins	brakes
un frère	brother
les frites	fries
froid	cold (temperature)
le fromage	cheese
le fromage blanc	cream cheese
les fruits	fruit
gagner	to earn
des gants	gloves
un gant de cuisine	oven mitt
un garçon	boy
la gare	train station
la gare de métro	subway station
garer (la voiture)	to park
la gare routière	bus station
le gâteau	cake
geler	freeze
la gencive	gum

le genou	knee
gentil	kind
un gérant	manager
la glace	ice cream
le golf	golf
une gomme	eraser
le goûter	snack
grand	tall
le grand magasin	department store
une grand-mère	grandmother
un grand-père	grandfather
le grenier	attic
un grille-pain	toaster
la grippe	flu
gris	grey
gros	fat
le guichet	counter, window
un guichet automatique bancaire (GAB)	ATM machine
la guitare	guitar
un haricot	bean
des hémorroïdes	hemorrhoids
heureux	happy
hindou	Hindu
hiver	winter
le hockey	hockey
un homme	man
honteux	ashamed
l'hôpital	hospital
l'hôtel	hotel
une hôtesse de l'air	stewardess
huit	eight
humide	humid
il	he, it

il y a	there is, there are
l'immigration	immigration
impatient	impatient
un imperméable	raincoat
une imprimante	printer
l'imprimé	form
indien(ne)	Indian
infecté	infected
un infirmier	nurse
(une infirmière)	
un ingénieur	engineer
une inondation	flood
inquiet	worried
insomniaque	insomniac
intelligent	smart
intéressant	interesting
l'iode	iodine
irlandais(e)	Irish
italien(ne)	Italian
la jambe	leg
le jambon	ham
janvier	January
japonais(e)	Japanese
le jardin	garden, yard
jardiner	to garden
jaune	yellow
un jean	jeans
jeudi	Thursday
le jogging	jogging
joli	good-looking
jolie	pretty
la joue	cheek
jouer à	to play (game, sport)
jouer de	to play (music)

un journal	newspaper
juillet	July
juin	June
une jupe	skirt
un jupon	half slip
le jus	juice
un kilogramme (un kilo)	kilogram
un kiosque	newsstand
lâche	cowardly
laid	ugly
laisser un message	to leave a message
le lait	milk
la laitue	lettuce
une lampe	lamp
le lapin	rabbit
le lavabo	sink (bathroom)
se laver	to wash (oneself)
un lave-vaisselle	dishwasher
la lecture	reading
une lettre	letter
la lèvre	lip
licencier	to lay off
la lime à ongles	nail file
lire	to read
un lit	bed
un litre	liter
un livre	book
une livre	pound
le logement	accommodations
loin (de)	far (from)
long	long
lourd	heavy
lundi	Monday
la lune de miel	honeymoon

des lunettes	eyeglasses
des lunettes de soleil	sunglasses
la lutte	wrestling
lutter	to wrestle, to fight
un lycée	high school
la mâchoire	jaw
Madame	Ma'am, Mrs.
Mademoiselle	Miss
mai	May
la main	hand
la maison	house
un magasin	store
le magasin de confection	clothing store
un magazine	magazine
un maillot (de bain)	bathing suit
un maillot de corps	undershirt
le maïs	corn
le mal de mer	seasickness
malade	sick
le mandat	money order
manger	to eat
un manteau	coat
le maquillage	make-up
se maquiller	to put on make-up
le marché	outdoor market
mardi	Tuesday
un mari	husband
le mariage	wedding
se marier avec	to get married
une marmite	pot
marocain(e)	Moroccan
marron	brown
mars	March
le mascara	mascara

mauvais	bad (weather)
la mayonnaise	mayonnaise
un mécanicien	mechanic
méchant	mean
un médecin	doctor
le menu	fixed-price meal
merci (bien/beaucoup)	thank you (very much)
mercredi	Wednesday
une mère	mother
le métro	subway
mexicain(e)	Mexican
mille	one thousand
mille fois merci	bless you! (thank you so much)
un mille	mile
un milliard	billion
un million	one million
mince	thin
une minijupe	miniskirt
un miroir	mirror
un mobile	cell phone
une mobylette	moped
moche	ugly
la molaire	molar
la monnaie	change
Monsieur	Mr., Sir
le montant	amount, total, sum
une montre	watch
une moquette	carpet
une moto	motorcycle
un mouchoir	handkerchief
des moufles	mittens
la mousse au chocolat	chocolate mousse
la moutarde	mustard
un mur	wall

une mûre	blackberry
le musée	museum
la musique	music
une myrtille	blueberry
nager	to swim
naïf	naive
la natation	swimming
une navette	shuttle
navré	sorry, distressed
ne . . . pas	not
néerlandais(e)	Dutch
neige	snow
neiger	snow (verb)
nerveux	nervous
neuf	nine, new
un neveu	nephew
le nez	nose
une nièce	niece
les noces	wedding
noir	black
noisette	hazelnut
non	no
nord	north
un noeud papillon	bow tie
novembre	November
la Novocaïne	Novocain
se noyer	to be drowning
nuageux	cloudy
un numéro de téléphone	phone number
octobre	October
un oeil (des yeux)	eye(s)
l'oeuf	egg
un oignon	onion
un oncle	uncle

ondulé	wavy
un ongle	fingernail
onze	eleven
l'opéra	opera
orageux	stormy
orange	orange (color)
une orange	orange
l'orchestre	orchestra
un ordinateur	computer
une oreille	ear
un oreiller	pillow
un orteil	toe
ou	or
où	where
Où est . . . ?	Where is . . . ?
ouest	west
oui	yes
ouvert	outgoing, open
ouvrez la bouche	open your mouth
le pain	bread
le pain complet	wholegrain bread
le pain de seigle	rye bread
un pamplemousse	grapefruit
un pantalon	pants
le papier	paper
un paquet	package
par avion	air mail
par express	special delivery
un parapluie	umbrella
le parc	park
pardon	pardon me
un pare-brise	windshield
paresseux	lazy
le parfum	perfume

le parking	parking lot/garage
un passager	passenger
un passeport	passport
les pâtes	pasta
patient	patient
le patin à roulettes	rollerskating
le patinage	skating
le patio	patio
la pâtisserie	pastry shop
patriotique	patriotic
payer	to pay
un péage	toll
une pêche	peach
la pêche	fishing
pêcher	to fish
le peigne	comb
une peinture	painting
un pendentif	pendant
la pénicilline	penicillin
perdre	to lose
un père	father
petit	short (height)
le petit-déjeuner	breakfast
une petite annonce	classified ad
une petit-fille	granddaughter
un petit-fils	grandson
les petits pois	peas
la pharmacie	pharmacy
un(e) pharmacien(ne)	pharmacist
les phares	headlights
le piano	piano
la pièce	room
une pièce (de monnaie)	coin
un pied	foot

le pilote	pilot
la pince à ongles	nail clippers
la pince à épiler	tweezers
une piqûre	injection
la piscine	pool
un placard	closet
la place	seat
le plafond	ceiling
une planche à découper	cutting board
le plat principal	main course
un plombage	filling
un plombier	plumber
la plongée	diving
plus	more, very
une poêle	frying pan
le poids	weight
le poignet	wrist
une poire	pear
le poisson	fish
la poissonnerie	fish store
la poitrine	chest
le poivre	pepper
un policier	police officer
polonais(e)	Polish
une pomme	apple
la pomme de terre	potato
un pompier	fireman
le porc	pork
le porche	porch
une porte	door, gate
un porte-documents	briefcase
un portefeuille	wallet
portugais(e)	Portuguese
la poste	post office

la poste restante	general delivery, hold mail
un pot	cup, jar
le potage	soup
le pouce	thumb, inch
le poulet	chicken
pour	for
le pourboire	tip
pourquoi	why
la première classe	first class
le premier étage	second floor (US)
près (de)	near (to)
pressé	rushed, in a hurry
printemps	spring
le prix	price
les produits laitiers	dairy products
un professeur	teacher
provisoire	temporary
une prune	plum
les P.T.T.	post office
un pull	sweater
un pupitre	student desk
un pyjama	pajamas
le quai	platform
quand	when
quarante	forty
quatorze	fourteen
quatre	four
qui	who
quinze	fifteen
quoi	what
raccrocher	to hang up
le radis	radish
raffiné	sophisticated
raide	straight (hair)

un raisin	grape
la randonnée	hiking
rappeler	to call back
le rasage	shaving
se raser	to shave
le rasoir	razor
le rasoir électrique	shaver
ravi	delighted
la réception des bagages	baggage claim
un(e) réceptionniste	receptionist
une recette	recipe
recommandé	registered
un reçu	receipt
la réexpédition	forwarding
un réfrigérateur	refrigerator
regarder la télé	to watch TV
regarder un film	to watch a movie
régler le compte	to pay the bill
un relevé de compte	bank statement
remplacer	to replace
le rendement	yield
renvoyer	to fire
le repas	meal
un répondeur téléphonique	answering machine
un responsable	manager
le restaurant	restaurant
retirer	to withdraw
un réveil	alarm clock
le rez-de-chaussée	first floor (US)
un rhume des foins	hay fever
un rideau	curtain
rien	nothing
rincer	to rinse
le riz	rice

une robe	dress
le rosbif	roast beef
rose	pink
une rose	rose
rouge	red
le rouge à lèvres	lipstick
un rouleau à pâtisserie	rolling pin
rouler	to drive
roux	red (hair)
un ruban	ribbon
la rue	street
russe	Russian
un sac à dos	backpack
un sac à main	purse
saigner	to bleed
les saisons	seasons
la salade	salad
la salle	room
la salle à manger	dining room
la salle de bains	bathroom
une salle de classe	classroom
la salle de séjour	den
le salon	living room
salut	hi, bye
samedi	Saturday
des sandales	sandals
sans préjugés	open-minded
le saucisson	sausage
le savon	soap
le saxophone	saxophone
la séance	showing, time
un(e) secrétaire	secretary
seize	sixteen
le sel	salt

sénégalais(e)	Senegalese
sept	seven
septembre	September
sérieux	serious
un serveur	waiter
une serveuse	waitress
service compris	tip included
le service de lessive	laundry service
service non compris	tip not included
une serviette	napkin, towel
le shampooing	shampoo
un short	shorts
si	yes (in response to a question posed in the negative)
signer	to sign
s'il vous/te plaît	please
la sinusite	sinusitis
six	six
le skate	skateboarding
le ski	skiing
un smoking	tuxedo
snob	snobbish
une soeur	sister
soixante	sixty
soixante-dix	seventy
le sol	floor
le solde	balance
du soleil	sunny
solitaire	lonely
sonner	to ring
sortir avec	to date
une soucoupe	saucer
la soupe	soup
le sous-sol	basement

un soutien-gorge	bra
sous-titré	subtitled
sous-vêtements	underwear
un spectacle	show, performance
sportif	athletic
la station de métro	subway station
la station de taxi	taxi stand
stationner	to park
une station-service	gas station
un steward	steward
studieux	studious
stupide	stupid
un stylo	pen
le sucre	sugar
sud	south
suisse	Swiss
un surligneur	highlighter
sympathique (sympa)	nice
la symphonie	symphony
un tabac	tobacco store
une table	table
un tableau	chalkboard
des taches de rousseur	freckles
un tailleur	suit (woman's)
une tante	aunt
un tapis	rug
taquin	playful
la tarte	pie
une tasse	cup
le taux de change	exchange rate
le taux d'intérêt	interest rate
un taxi	taxi
un tee-shirt	T-shirt
la teinturerie	dry cleaner

la télé	TV
un télécopieur	fax machine
un téléphone	telephone
téléphoner à	to call (phone)
la télévision	television
le tennis	tennis
des tennis	sneakers
la tension artérielle	blood pressure
la tête	head
le thé	tea
le théâtre	theater
un timbre	stamp
timbres en gros	bulk stamps
timide	shy
le tir à l'arc	archery
la toilette	toilet
les toilettes	restroom
la tomate	tomato
la tonalité	dial tone
un torchon	dish towel
toucher un chèque	to cash a check
tourner	to turn
tousser	to cough
tout droit	straight ahead
le train	train
tranquille	calm
une transmission automatique	automatic transmission
le transport	transportation
travailler	to work
travailleur	hard-working
traverser	to cross
treize	thirteen
trente	thirty
triste	sad

trois	three
une trombone	paper clip
la trompette	trumpet
un	one, a, an
une université	college, university
Urgence !	Emergency!
la vanille	vanilla
le veau	veal
végétarien(ne)	vegetarian
un vélo	bike
vendre	to sell
vendredi	Friday
du vent	windy
le vernis à ongles	nail polish
un verre	glass
un verre gradué	measuring cup
vert	green
le vertige	dizzy
un veston de sport	sport jacket
des vêtements	clothes
veuillez (in front of a verb)	please
le vin	wine
vingt	twenty
le violon	violin
un visa	visa
le visage	face
la voile	sailing
violet	purple
voici	this is
une voiture	car
un vol	flight, theft
le volant	steering wheel
le volley(ball)	volleyball
vomir	to throw up

vouloir	to want
le yaourt	yogurt
les yeux (un oeil)	eyes (eye)

Appendix B
English to French Dictionary

abscess	*un abcès*
accident	*un accident*
accommodations	*le logement*
to ache all over	*avoir mal partout*
actor	*un acteur*
actress	*une actrice*
adding machine	*une machine à calculer*
address	*une adresse*
African	*africain(e)*
after-dinner drink	*le digestif*
air conditioner	*un climatiseur*
air mail	*par avion*
airline	*une compagnie aérienne*
airplane	*un avion*
airport	*un aéroport*
alarm clock	*un réveil*
Algerian	*algérien(ne)*
allergic to	*allergique à*
almond	*l'amande*
amazing	*étonnant*
amount, total, sum	*le montant*
ambulance	*une ambulance*
anchovies	*les anchois*
and	*et*
angry	*fâché*
ankle	*la cheville*
anniversary	*l'anniversaire*
annoyed	*ennuyé*
answering machine	*un répondeur téléphonique*
appetizers	*les hors-d'oeuvre*
apple	*une pomme*
apricot	*un abricot*
April	*avril*
Arabic	*arabe*

archery	*le tir à l'arc*
arm	*le bras*
arrivals	*les arrivées*
arthritis	*de l'arthrite*
artichoke	*un artichaut*
artist	*un(e) artiste*
ashamed	*honteux*
Asian	*asiatique*
asparagus	*les asperges*
aspirin	*une aspirine*
asthmatic	*asthmatique*
athletic	*sportif*
ATM card	*une carte bancaire*
ATM machine	*un guichet automatique bancaire (GAB)*
attic	*le grenier*
August	*août*
aunt	*une tante*
Australian	*australien(ne)*
automatic transmission	*une transmission automatique*
autumn	*automne*
baby tooth	*la dent de lait*
back	*le dos*
backpack	*un sac à dos*
bad	*mal, mauvais*
bad weather	*mauvais temps*
baggage	*les bagages*
baggage claim	*la réception des bagages*
baker	*un boulanger (une boulangère)*
bakery	*la boulangerie*
baking dish	*une casserole*
balance	*le solde*
balcony	*le balcon*
banana	*une banane*

bank	*une banque*
bank card	*une carte bancaire*
bank statement	*un relevé de compte*
barber	*le coiffeur*
barrette	*une barrette*
barrister, lawyer	*un(e) avocat(e)*
baseball	*le base-ball*
basement	*le sous-sol*
basketball	*le basket(-ball)*
bathing suit	*un maillot (de bain)*
bathroom	*la salle de bains*
bathtub	*une baignoire*
to be	*être*
bean	*un haricot*
bed	*un lit*
bedroom	*la chambre*
beer	*la bière*
Belgian	*belge*
belt	*une ceinture*
bicycle	*une bicyclette*
bike	*un vélo*
biking	*le cyclisme*
bikini	*un bikini*
bill	*l'addition*
billion	*un milliard*
binder	*un classeur*
black	*noir*
blackberry	*une mûre*
to bleed	*saigner*
bless you (after a sneeze)	*à vos/tes souhaits*
blond	*blond(e)*
blood pressure	*la tension artérielle*
blouse	*une chemise*
blue	*bleu*

blueberry	*une myrtille*
to blunder	*faire une gaffe*
blusher	*le fard à joues*
to board	*embarquer*
boarding pass	*la carte d'embarquement*
boat	*un bateau*
to bolt the door	*mettre le verrou*
book	*un livre*
bookshelf	*une étagère*
boots	*des bottes*
bored	*ennuyé*
boring	*ennuyeux*
boss	*le chef*
bottle	*une bouteille*
bow tie	*un noeud papillon*
bowl	*un bol*
boxer shorts	*un caleçon*
boxing	*la boxe*
boy	*un garçon*
boyfriend	*un copain*
bra	*un soutien-gorge*
bracelet	*un bracelet*
brake lights	*les feux de stop*
brakes	*les freins*
brave	*courageux*
Brazilian	*brésilien(ne)*
bread	*le pain*
to break (arm, leg)	*se casser (le bras, la jambe)*
breakfast	*le petit-déjeuner*
briefcase	*un porte-documents*
to bring out	*mettre en relief*
broken tooth	*une dent cassée*
broken-down	*en panne*
brooch	*une broche*

brother	*un frère*
brown	*marron*
brown (hair)	*brun*
brown bread	*le pain bis*
to brush one's hair	*se brosser les cheveux*
to brush one's teeth	*se brosser les dents*
bubble bath	*le bain moussant*
bulk stamps	*timbres en gros*
bus	*l'autobus*
bus station	*la gare routière*
bus stop	*l'arrêt du bus*
busy	*occupé(e)*
butcher	*un boucher*
butcher shop	*la boucherie*
butter	*le beurre*
buttermilk	*le babeurre*
to buy	*acheter*
bye	*salut*
cake	*le gâteau*
calculator	*une calculatrice*
to call	*appeler, téléphoner à*
to call back	*rappeler*
calm	*tranquille*
can, box, tin	*une boîte*
Canadian	*canadien(ne)*
candy	*des bonbons*
candy store	*la confiserie*
car	*une auto, une voiture*
carpenter	*un charpentier*
carpet	*une moquette*
carrot	*la carotte*
carry-on luggage	*les bagages à main*
cart	*un chariot*
cash	*des espèces*

to cash a check	*encaisser, toucher un chèque*
cash dispenser	*un guichet automatique bancaire (GAB)*
cashier	*un caissier (une caissière)*
cauliflower	*le chou-fleur*
cavity	*une carie*
ceiling	*le plafond*
celery	*le céleri*
cell phone	*un mobile*
CEO	*le directeur général*
certified check	*un chèque certifié*
chair	*une chaise*
chalk	*une craie*
chalkboard	*un tableau*
change	*la monnaie*
to change money (into Euros)	*changer de l'argent (en Euros)*
charm bracelet	*un bracelet à breloques*
check, bill	*l'addition*
to check bags	*enregistrer (les bagages)*
checkbook	*un carnet de chèques*
checked luggage	*les bagages enregistrés*
check-in	*l'enregistrement*
checking account	*un compte-chèques*
cheek	*la joue*
cheers	*à votre/ta santé*
cheese	*le fromage*
cherry	*une cerise*
chess	*les échecs*
chest	*la poitrine*
chicken	*le poulet*
Chinese	*chinois(e)*
chocolate	*le chocolat*
church	*l'église*

civil servant	*un(e) fonctionnaire*
classified ad	*une petite annonce*
classroom	*une salle de classe*
closet	*une armoire, un placard*
clothes	*des vêtements*
clothing store	*le magasin de confection*
cloudy	*nuageux*
coach class	*la classe touriste*
coat	*un manteau*
cocktail	*un apéritif*
coffee	*le café*
coin	*une pièce (de monnaie)*
cold (illness)	*un rhume*
cold (temperature)	*froid*
collect call	*un appel en P.C.V.*
college	*une université*
comb	*le peigne*
compact car	*une voiture compacte*
to compel	*mettre dans l'obligation de*
computer	*un ordinateur*
conditioner	*le baume démêlant*
confident	*assuré*
confused	*désorienté*
constipated	*constipé*
contract	*un contrat*
convertible	*une voiture décapotable*
cook	*le/la chef*
to cook	*cuisiner, faire la cuisine*
cookbook	*un livre de cuisine*
cookie	*le biscuit*
cooking	*la cuisine*
cool	*frais*
copy machine	*une photocopieuse*
corn	*le maïs*

couch	*un canapé*
to cough	*tousser*
to count	*compter*
counter, window	*le guichet*
country bread	*le pain de campagne*
course	*un cours*
cousin	*un(e) cousin(e)*
cowardly	*lâche*
crash	*une collision*
cream	*la crème*
cream cheese	*le fromage blanc*
credit card	*une carte de crédit*
croissant	*un croissant*
to cross	*traverser*
cross-country skiing	*le ski de randonnée, de fond*
crown	*la couronne*
cucumber	*le concombre*
cufflink	*un bouton de manchette*
cummerbund	*une ceinture*
cup	*une tasse*
curly	*bouclé*
currency exchange	*un bureau de change*
curtain	*un rideau*
custard	*la crème brûlée*
customs	*la douane*
cutting board	*une planche à découper*
dairy products	*les produits laitiers*
dance, dancing	*la danse*
to dance	*danser*
dark blue	*bleu foncé*
to date	*sortir avec*
daughter/a girl	*une fille*
December	*décembre*
to declare	*déclarer*

delighted	*ravi*
den	*la salle de séjour*
dental floss	*le fil dentaire*
dentist	*un(e) dentiste*
deodorant	*le déodorant*
department store	*le grand magasin*
departures	*les départs*
to deposit (into an account)	*déposer (sur un compte)*
desk	*un bureau, un pupitre*
dessert	*le dessert*
diabetic	*diabétique*
to dial a number	*composer un numéro*
dial tone	*la tonalité*
diarrhea	*la diarrhée*
dictionary	*un dictionnaire*
dimples	*des fossettes*
dining room	*la salle à manger*
dinner	*le dîner*
dish towel	*un torchon*
dishrack	*un égouttoir*
dishwasher	*un lave-vaisselle*
distressed, sorry	*navré*
diving	*la plongée*
dizzy	*le vertige*
to do, make	*faire*
doctor	*un médecin*
don't mention it	*il n'y a pas de quoi*
door	*une porte*
double bed	*un grand lit*
doubtful	*douteux*
down	*en bas*
downhill skiing	*le ski de descente, de piste*
dress	*une robe*

dresser	*une commode*
to drink	*boire*
to drive	*conduire, rouler*
driver	*un conducteur*
drugstore	*la droguerie*
dry cleaner	*la teinturerie*
dubbed	*doublé*
Dutch	*néerlandais(e)*
duty-free	*une boutique hors taxes*
ear	*une oreille*
earache	*mal à l'oreille*
early	*en avance*
to earn	*gagner*
earring	*une boucle d'oreille*
east	*est*
to eat	*manger*
economy car	*une voiture économie*
economy class	*la classe touriste*
egg	*l'oeuf*
eggplant	*une aubergine*
Egyptian	*égyptien(ne)*
eight	*huit*
eighteen	*dix-huit*
eighty	*quatre-vingts*
elbow	*le coude*
electrician	*un électricien*
elevator	*un ascenseur*
eleven	*onze*
e-mail	*le courriel*
embarassed	*confus*
Emergency!	*Urgence !*
employee	*un(e) employé(e)*
engagement	*les fiançailles*
engineer	*un ingénieur*

English	*anglais(e)*
to enhance	*mettre en relief*
enjoy your meal	*bon appétit !*
envelope	*une enveloppe*
eraser	*une gomme*
espresso	*un express*
European	*européen(ne)*
exchange rate	*le taux de change*
excuse me	*excusez-moi*
exhausted	*épuisé*
explosion	*une explosion*
Express mail	*Chronopost*
eye(s)	*un oeil (des yeux)*
eyeglasses	*des lunettes*
eyeshadow	*le fard à paupières*
face	*le visage*
to face up to	*faire face à*
to faint	*s'évanouir*
far (from)	*loin (de)*
farewell	*adieu*
fat	*gros*
father	*un père*
fax machine	*un télécopieur*
February	*février*
fees	*les frais*
to fetch, get	*aller chercher*
fever	*la fièvre*
fiancé(e)	*un(e) fiancé(e)*
fifteen	*quinze*
fifty	*cinquante*
file folder	*une chemise*
filing cabinet	*un classeur*
to fill up	*faire le plein*
filling	*un plombage*

fine	*ça va*
finger	*le doigt*
fingernail	*un ongle*
fire	*un feu*
Fire!	*Au feu !*
to fire (someone)	*renvoyer (quelqu'un)*
fireman	*un pompier*
first class	*la première classe*
first floor (US), ground floor	*le rez-de-chaussée*
fish	*le poisson*
to fish	*pêcher*
fish store	*la poissonnerie*
fishing	*la pêche*
five	*cinq*
fixed-price meal	*le menu*
flan	*la crème caramel*
Flemmish	*flamand*
flight	*un vol*
flight attendant	*un steward, une hôtesse de l'air*
flood	*une inondation*
floor	*le sol*
flowers	*des fleurs*
flu	*la grippe*
flute	*la flûte*
foggy	*du brouillard*
foot	*un pied*
football	*le football américain*
for	*pour*
fork	*une fourchette*
form	*l'imprimé*
forty	*quarante*
forwarding	*la réexpédition*
foundation	*la base (de maquillage)*

four	*quatre*
fourteen	*quatorze*
freckles	*des taches de rousseur*
freezer	*un congélateur*
freeze	*geler*
French	*français(e)*
Friday	*vendredi*
friend	*un(e) ami(e)*
friendly	*amical*
fries	*les frites*
front tooth	*l'incisive*
frostbite	*des engelures*
fruit	*les fruits*
frying pan	*une poêle*
funny	*drôle*
garden, yard	*le jardin*
to garden	*jardiner, faire du jardinage*
gas, petrol	*de l'essence*
gas pedal	*un accélérateur*
gas station	*une station-service*
gate	*une porte (aéroport)*
general delivery	*la poste restante*
German	*allemand(e)*
to get, fetch	*aller chercher*
to get engaged	*se fiancer à*
to get married	*se marier avec*
girl	*une fille*
girlfriend	*une copine*
to give	*donner*
to give a reason	*rendre raison*
to give up	*donner sa langue au chat*
to give thanks to	*rendre grâce à*
glass	*un verre*
glasses	*des lunettes*

to glorify	*rendre gloire à*
gloves	*des gants*
to go	*aller*
Go ahead!	*Allez-y !*
to go, move	*circuler*
to go, walk around	*faire le tour de*
to go away	*s'en aller*
to go on foot	*aller à pied*
to go shopping	*faire les courses*
golf	*le golf*
good	*bon(ne)*
Good evening	*Bonsoir*
Good night	*Bonne nuit*
Good-bye	*Au revoir*
granddaughter	*une petit-fille*
grandfather	*un grand-père*
grandmother	*une grand-mère*
grandson	*un petit-fils*
grape	*un raisin*
grapefruit	*un pamplemousse*
gray	*gris*
green	*vert*
grocery store	*l'épicerie*
guitar	*la guitare*
gums	*la gencive*
gunshot	*un coup de feu*
hair	*les cheveux*
hairbrush	*la brosse à cheveux*
hairdresser	*le coiffeur*
half slip	*un jupon*
hall	*le couloir*
hallway	*le couloir*
ham	*le jambon*
hand	*la main*

handkerchief	*un mouchoir*
handsome	*beau*
to hang up	*raccrocher*
happy	*heureux*
hard-working	*travailleur*
hat	*un chapeau*
to have	*avoir*
hay fever	*un rhume des foins*
hazel	*noisette*
head	*la tête*
headache	*mal à la tête*
headlights	*les phares*
heartburn	*des brûlures d'estomac*
heavy	*lourd*
Hello	*Bonjour*
Hello? (on the phone)	*Allô ?*
help	*de l'assistance*
Help!	*Au secours !*
hemorrhoids	*des hémorroïdes*
Hi	*Salut*
high beams	*les feux de route*
high school	*un lycée*
high-heeled shoes	*des chaussures à hauts talons*
highlighter	*un surligneur*
highway	*une autoroute*
to hike	*faire de la randonnée*
hiking	*la randonnée*
Hindu	*hindou*
to hire	*embaucher*
to hitchhike	*faire de l'auto-stop*
hitchhiking	*l'auto-stop*
hockey	*le hockey*
hold mail	*la poste restante*
homework	*des devoirs*

honeymoon	*la lune de miel*
hospital	*l'hôpital*
hot	*chaud*
hotel	*un hôtel*
hotel room	*une chambre*
house	*la maison*
how	*comment*
How are you?	*Ça va ?*
How much is it?	*C'est combien ?*
humid	*humide*
hundred	*cent*
to hunt	*(aller) chasser*
to hunt for	*faire la chasse à*
hunting	*la chasse*
to hurt	*avoir mal, faire mal à*
husband	*un mari, un époux*
hyper(active)	*excité*
ice cream	*la glace*
immigration	*l'immigration*
impatient	*impatient*
in a hurry	*pressé*
in back of	*en arrière de*
in economy class	*en classe touriste*
in first class	*en première classe*
in front of	*en avant de*
inbox	*le courrier arrivé*
inch	*un pouce*
Indian	*indien(ne)*
infected	*infecté*
injection	*une piqûre*
insomnia	*insomniaque*
insured	*assuré*
to intend to	*avoir l'intention de*
interest rate	*le taux d'intérêt*

interesting	*intéressant*
iodine	*l'iode*
Irish	*irlandais(e)*
Italian	*italien(ne)*
jacket	*un blouson*
jam	*la confiture*
January	*janvier*
Japanese	*japonais(e)*
jar, cup	*un pot*
jaw	*la mâchoire*
jeans	*un jean*
jet lagged	*fatigué dû au décalage horaire*
jewelry	*des bijoux*
jogging	*le jogging*
juice	*le jus*
July	*juillet*
June	*juin*
to kick	*donner un coup de pied*
kilogram	*un kilogramme de*
kind	*gentil*
kitchen	*la cuisine*
knee	*le genou*
knife	*un couteau*
lamb	*l'agneau*
to land	*atterrir*
lamp	*une lampe*
late	*en retard*
laundromat	*la blanchisserie*
laundry service	*le service de blanchisserie*
lawyer, barrister	*un(e) avocat(e)*
to lay off	*licencier*
to lay down flat	*mettre à plat*
lazy	*paresseux*
to leave a message	*laisser un message*

left	*(à) gauche*
leg	*la jambe*
lemon	*un citron*
lemonade	*le citron pressé*
Let's go!	*Allons-y !*
letter	*une lettre*
lettuce	*la laitue*
light blue	*bleu clair*
lime	*un citron vert*
lip	*la lèvre*
lipstick	*le rouge à lèvres*
to listen to music	*écouter (de) la musique*
liter	*un litre*
living room	*le salon*
loan	*un emprunt*
local anesthesia	*une anesthésie locale*
lonely	*solitaire*
long	*long*
to lose	*perdre*
lover	*un(e) amant(e)*
lunch	*le déjeuner*
luxury car	*une voiture luxe*
Ma'am, Mrs.	*Madame*
magazine	*un magazine*
maid	*une femme de chambre*
mail	*le courrier*
mailbox	*une boîte aux lettres*
main course	*le plat principal*
to make, do	*faire*
to make the bed	*faire le lit*
make-up	*le maquillage*
make-up remover	*le démaquillant*
man	*un homme*
manager	*un gérant, un responsable*

map	*une carte*
March	*mars*
marriage	*le mariage*
to marry	*s'épouser*
mascara	*le mascara*
May (month)	*mai*
mayonnaise	*la mayonnaise*
meal	*le repas*
mean	*méchant*
measuring cup	*un verre gradué*
measuring spoon	*une cuiller à mesurer*
mechanic	*un mécanicien*
medium-rare	*à point*
to meet	*faire la connaissance de*
(for the first time)	
menu	*la carte*
Mexican	*mexicain(e)*
microwave	*un four à micro-ondes*
midnight	*minuit*
mid-size car	*une voiture intermédiaire*
mile (1.6 km)	*un mille*
milk	*le lait*
million	*un million*
miniskirt	*une minijupe*
mirror	*un miroir*
Miss	*Mademoiselle*
mistake	*une erreur*
mittens	*des moufles*
moisturizer	*la crème hydratante*
Monday	*lundi*
money	*de l'argent*
money exchange	*le bureau de change*
money order	*le mandat*
moped	*une mobylette*

more, very	*plus*
Moroccan	*marocain(e)*
mother	*une mère*
motion sickness	*le mal des transports*
motorbike	*une moto*
mouth	*la bouche*
mouthwash	*l'eau dentifrice*
movie	*le film*
movie theater	*le cinéma*
Mr.	*Monsieur*
Mrs., Ma'am	*Madame*
muffler	*un cache-nez*
museum	*le musée*
mushroom	*le champignon*
music	*la musique*
mustard	*la moutarde*
nail clippers	*la pince à ongles*
nail file	*la lime à ongles*
nail polish	*le vernis à ongles*
nail polish remover	*le dissolvant*
naive	*naïf*
napkin	*une serviette*
near (to)	*près (de)*
necessary	*nécessaire*
neck	*le cou*
necklace	*un collier*
to need	*avoir besoin de*
nephew	*un neveu*
nervous	*nerveux*
newspaper	*un journal*
newsstand	*un kiosque*
next to	*à côté de*
nice	*sympathique (or sympa)*
nice (weather)	*beau*

niece	*une nièce*
nightgown	*une chemise de nuit*
nine	*neuf*
nineteen	*dix-neuf*
ninety	*quatre-vingt-dix*
no	*non*
noon	*midi*
north	*nord*
nose	*le nez*
note, bill, paper money	*un billet*
notebook	*un cahier*
nothing	*rien*
November	*novembre*
Novocain	*la Novocaïne*
nurse	*un infirmier (une infirmière)*
obvious	*évident*
October	*octobre*
office	*un bureau*
OK	*d'accord*
on the way	*en route*
one	*un*
one hundred	*cent*
one million	*un million*
one more time	*encore une fois*
one thousand	*mille*
one-way ticket	*un billet aller*
onion	*un oignon*
to open	*ouvrir*
open-minded	*sans préjugés*
opera	*l'opéra*
to oppose	*faire face à*
or	*ou*
orange	*une orange*
orange (color)	*orange*

orchestra	*l'orchestre*
to order	*commander*
other	*autre*
outbox	*le courrier départ*
outdoor market	*le marché*
outgoing	*ouvert*
oven	*un four*
oven mitt	*un gant de cuisine*
to pack	*faire les bagages, valises*
package	*un colis, un paquet*
painting	*une peinture*
pajamas	*un pyjama*
panties	*une culotte*
pants	*un pantalon*
pantyhose	*un collant*
paper	*le papier*
paper clip	*un trombone*
paper money, note, bill	*un billet*
pardon me	*pardon*
park	*le parc*
to park	*stationner*
parking lot/garage	*le parking*
to pass	*doubler*
passenger	*un passager*
passport	*un passeport*
pasta	*les pâtes*
pastry shop	*la pâtisserie*
patient	*patient(e)*
patio	*le patio*
patriotic	*patriotique*
to pay	*payer*
to pay a visit	*faire une visite, rendre visite à*
to pay attention to	*faire attention à*
to pay for	*mettre de l'argent pour*

to pay the bill	*régler le compte*
peach	*une pêche*
peanut	*l'arachide, la cacahuète*
pear	*une poire*
peas	*petits pois*
pets	*les animaux*
pharmacist	*un(e) pharmacien(ne)*
pharmacy	*la pharmacie*
phone book	*un annuaire*
phone booth	*une cabine téléphonique*
phone number	*un numéro de téléphone*
piano	*le piano*
to pick up (the phone)	*décrocher*
pie	*la tarte*
pillow	*un oreiller*
pilot	*le pilote*
pin	*une épingle*
pink	*rose*
plane ticket	*le billet d'avion*
plans	*des projets*
plate	*une assiette*
platform	*le quai*
to play music	*jouer de la musique*
playful	*taquin*
please	*s'il vous / te plaît*
Please hold	*Ne quittez pas*
plum	*une prune*
plumber	*un plombier*
police officer	*un policier*
police station	*le commissariat*
Polish	*polonais(e)*
pool	*la piscine*
porch	*le porche*
pork	*le porc*

pork butcher	*la charcuterie*
Portuguese	*portugais(e)*
post card	*une carte postale*
post office	*la poste, les P.T.T*
postal checking account	*un compte chèque postal (CCP)*
poster	*une affiche*
pot	*une marmite*
potato	*la pomme de terre*
pound	*une livre de*
to pout	*faire la moue*
pregnant	*enceinte*
present	*un cadeau*
to pretend to	*faire semblant de*
pretty	*belle, jolie*
price	*le prix*
printer	*une imprimante*
problem	*problème*
to pull out, remove	*arracher*
purple	*violet*
purse	*un sac à main*
to put money into	*mettre de l'argent dans*
to put on make-up	*se maquiller*
quarter	*le quart*
rabbit	*le lapin*
radish	*le radis*
raincoat	*un imperméable*
rare (meat)	*bleu*
raspberry	*une framboise*
razor	*le rasoir*
to read	*lire*
reading	*la lecture*
receipt	*un reçu*
receptionist	*un(e) réceptionniste*
recipe	*une recette*

recipient	*le destinataire*
red	*rouge*
red (hair)	*roux*
refrigerator	*un réfrigérateur*
registered	*recommandé*
regular gas	*essence ordinaire*
to repeat	*répéter*
to replace	*remplacer*
reservation	*une réservation*
restaurant	*le restaurant*
return receipt	*l'avis de réception*
ribbon	*un ruban*
rice	*le riz*
to ride in a car	*aller en voiture*
right	*(à) droit(e)*
ring	*une bague*
to ring	*sonner*
to rinse	*rincer*
roast beef	*le rosbif*
rollerskating	*le patin à roulettes, le roller*
rolling pin	*un rouleau à pâtisserie*
room	*la pièce, la salle*
root canal	*la dévitalisation*
round trip ticket	*un billet aller-retour*
rug	*un tapis*
to run errands	*faire les courses*
runny nose	*le nez qui coule*
rushed	*pressé*
Russian	*russe*
rye bread	*le pain de seigle*
sad	*triste*
sailing	*la voile*
salad	*la salade*
salt	*le sel*

sandals	*des sandales*
Saturday	*samedi*
saucer	*une soucoupe*
sausage	*le saucisson*
to save money, save up	*faire des économies*
savings account	*un compte d'épargne*
to say good-bye	*faire ses adieux*
saxophone	*le saxophone*
scared	*effrayé*
scarf	*un foulard*
school	*une école*
seasickness	*le mal de mer*
seasons	*les saisons*
seat	*la place*
second floor (US)	*le premier étage*
secretary	*un(e) secrétaire*
security check	*le contrôle de sécurité*
see you soon	*à bientôt*
see you tomorrow	*à demain*
to sell	*vendre*
sender	*l'expéditeur*
Senegalese	*sénégalais(e)*
September	*septembre*
serious	*sérieux*
to set the alarm	*mettre le réveil*
to set the table	*mettre la table*
seven	*sept*
seventeen	*dix-sept*
seventy	*soixante-dix*
Shall we go?	*On y va ?*
shameful	*honteux*
shampoo	*le shampooing*
to shave	*se raser*
shaver	*le rasoir électrique*

shaving	*le rasage*
shaving cream	*la crème à raser*
shawl	*un châle*
she	*elle*
sheet of paper	*une feuille de papier*
shelf	*une étagère*
shirt	*une chemise*
shoes	*des chaussures*
short (height)	*petit*
short (length)	*court*
shorts	*un short*
shoulder	*une épaule*
show, performance	*un spectacle*
shower	*la douche*
showing, time	*la séance*
shuttle	*une navette*
shy	*timide*
sick	*malade*
to sign	*signer*
sink (bathroom)	*le lavabo*
sink (kitchen)	*un évier*
sinusitis	*de la sinusite*
Sir	*Monsieur*
sister	*une soeur*
six	*six*
sixteen	*seize*
sixty	*soixante*
size	*la dimension, la taille*
skating	*le patinage*
to ski	*skier, faire du ski*
skiing	*le ski*
skirt	*une jupe*
to sleep in/late	*faire la grasse matinée*
slip	*une combinaison*

slowly	*lentement*
smart	*intelligent*
smoke	*fumer*
snack	*le goûter*
snails	*les escargots*
sneakers	*des tennis*
to sneeze	*éternuer*
snobbish	*snob*
to snow	*neiger*
soap	*le savon*
soccer	*le football, le foot*
socks	*des chaussettes*
sofa	*le canapé*
son	*un fils*
sophisticated	*raffiné*
sorry, distressed	*navré*
so-so	*comme ci, comme ça*
soup	*la soupe, le potage*
sourdough bread	*le pain au levain*
south	*sud*
Spanish	*espagnol(e)*
special delivery	*par express*
to spend	*dépenser*
to spend money	*dépenser*
spinach	*les épinards*
sponge	*une éponge*
spoon	*une cuiller*
sport jacket	*une veste de sport*
spring	*printemps*
stairway	*un escalier*
stamp	*un timbre*
staple	*une agrafe*
stapler	*une agrafeuse*
steak	*le bifteck*

steering wheel	*le volant*
stereo	*une chaîne stéréo*
stockings	*des bas*
stomach	*un estomac*
stomachache	*mal à l'estomac*
stop light	*le feu rouge*
stopover	*une escale*
stores	*les magasins*
stormy	*orageux*
stove	*une cuisinière*
straight (hair)	*raide*
straight ahead	*tout droit*
strawberry	*une fraise*
street	*la rue*
strong	*fort*
student	*un(e) étudiant(e)*
studious	*studieux*
study	*un bureau*
stupid	*stupide*
subtitled	*sous-titré*
subway	*le métro*
subway station	*la gare/station de métro*
sugar	*le sucre*
suit (man's)	*un costume*
suit (woman's)	*un tailleur*
to suit, to be becoming	*aller à quelqu'un*
to sulk	*faire la tête*
sum, amount, total	*le montant*
summer	*été*
sunburn	*coup de soleil*
Sunday	*dimanche*
sunglasses	*des lunettes de soleil*
sunny	*du soleil*
sure	*sûr*

sweater	*un pull*
to swim	*nager*
swimming	*la natation*
Swiss	*suisse*
symphony	*la symphonie*
table	*une table*
tablespoon	*une cuillère à soupe*
tall	*grand*
to take a trip	*faire un voyage*
to take off	*décoller*
tanned	*bronzé*
taxi	*un taxi*
taxi stand	*la station de taxi*
tea	*le thé*
teacher	*un professeur, un(e) enseignant(e)*
teaspoon	*une cuillère à thé*
teeth cleaning	*le détartrage*
telephone	*un téléphone*
television	*la télévision*
temporary	*provisoire*
ten	*dix*
ten to seven	*sept heures moins dix*
tennis	*le tennis*
terminal	*une aérogare*
test	*un examen*
thank you (very much)	*merci (bien/beaucoup)*
theater	*le théâtre*
theft	*le vol*
Thief!	*Au voleur !*
thin	*mince*
thing	*chose*
to think	*penser*
thirteen	*treize*
thirty	*trente*

this is	*voici*
thousand	*mille*
three	*trois*
to throw a party	*donner une fête*
to throw up	*vomir*
thumb	*le pouce*
Thursday	*jeudi*
tie	*une cravate*
tie pin	*une épingle de cravate*
tights	*un collant*
time	*le temps*
tip	*le pourboire*
tip included	*service compris*
tired	*fatigué*
toast	*le pain grillé*
toaster	*un grille-pain*
tobacco store	*un tabac*
toe	*un orteil*
toilet	*la toilette, les W.-C.,* les toilettes
toll	*un péage*
tomato	*la tomate*
tooth	*la dent*
toothache	*mal aux dents*
toothbrush	*la brosse à dents*
toothpaste	*le dentifrice*
total, amount, sum	*le montant*
towel	*la serviette*
traffic jam	*un embouteillage*
train	*le train*
train station	*la gare*
transportation	*le transport*
traveler's check	*un chèque de voyage*
trip	*une excursion*
truck	*un camion*

true	*vrai*
trumpet	*la trompette*
T-shirt	*un tee-shirt*
tub	*la baignoire, le bain*
Tuesday	*mardi*
turkey	*la dinde*
to turn	*tourner*
to turn on the radio, the news	*mettre la radio, les informations*
turn signal	*le clignotant*
tuxedo	*un smoking*
TV	*la télé*
tweezers	*la pince à épiler*
twelve	*douze*
twenty	*vingt*
two	*deux*
typewriter	*une machine à écrire*
ugly	*moche, laid*
umbrella	*un parapluie*
uncle	*un oncle*
undershirt	*un maillot de corps*
underwear	*un sous-vêtement*
unfriendly	*froid*
unleavened bread	*le pain azyme*
unlikely	*peu probable*
until next time	*à la prochaine*
up	*en haut*
upper tooth	*la dent du haut*
useful	*utile*
useless	*inutile*
vanilla	*la vanille*
veal	*le veau*
vegetarian	*végétarien(ne)*
violin	*le violon*

visa	*un visa*
to visit someone	*rendre visite à quelqu'un*
volleyball	*le volley(-ball)*
waiter	*un serveur*
waitress	*une serveuse*
walk	*promenade*
wall	*un mur*
wallet	*un portefeuille*
to want	*avoir envie de, vouloir*
to wash	*se laver*
to wash the dishes	*faire la vaisselle*
watch	*une montre*
to watch a movie	*regarder un film*
to watch out for	*faire attention à*
Watch out!	*Attention !*
water	*l'eau*
water skiing	*le ski nautique*
wavy	*ondulé*
weak	*faible*
wedding	*les noces, le mariage*
wedding ring	*une alliance*
Wednesday	*mercredi*
weight	*le poids*
to welcome	*faire bon accueil*
well done (meat)	*bien cuit*
west	*ouest*
what	*quoi*
What?	*Comment ?*
wheat	*le blé*
when	*quand*
where	*où*
Where is . . . ?	*Où est . . . ?*
white	*blanc*
who	*qui*

wholegrain bread	*le pain complet*
why	*pourquoi*
wife	*une femme, une épouse*
window	*une fenêtre*
windshield	*un pare-brise*
windshield wipers	*les essuie-glaces*
windy	*du vent*
wine	*le vin*
to wink at	*faire un clin d'oeil à*
winter	*hiver*
wisdom tooth	*la dent de sagesse*
to withdraw	*retirer*
woman	*une femme*
to work	*travailler*
worried	*inquiet*
to worship	*rendre un culte à*
to wrestle	*lutter*
wrestling	*la lutte*
wrist	*le poignet*
to write	*écrire*
writer	*un écrivain*
yard, garden	*le jardin*
yellow	*jaune*
yes	*oui*
yes (in reponse to a negative)	*si*
yield	*le rendement*
yogurt	*le yaourt*
you're welcome	*de rien*

Appendix C
Additional Resources

About the French Language, *✎http://french.about.com*
Website with information about every aspect of the French language, including lessons, quizzes, sound files, and a special section for beginning students.

Champs-Élysées **audiomagazine,** *✎web.champs-elysees. com/cemag*
Audiomagazine for intermediate and advanced French students with short features on diverse topics in current events and culture.

Les portes tordues, *✎www.home.thetwisteddoors.com*
Bilingual audiobook for beginning to intermediate students. Audio CD with bilingual transcript, vocabulary lists, grammar lessons, and quizzes.

Au Contraire! Figuring Out the French by Gilles Asselin and Ruth Mastron. Intercultural Press, ME, 2001.

The Everything® Learning French Book by Bruce Sallee and David Hebert. Adams Media, Avon MA, 2002.

French or Foe? by Polly Platt. Culture Crossings, Ltd., London, 1994.